Who Said School Administration Would Be Fun?

Coping With a New Emotional and Social Reality

Jane L. Sigford

CORWIN PRESS, INC.
A Sage Publications Company
Thousand Oaks, California

For information:

Corwin Press, Inc.
A Sage Publications Company
2455 Teller Road
Thousand Oaks, California 91320
E-mail: order@corwinpress.com

SAGE Publications Ltd.
6 Bonhill Street
London EC2A 4PU
United Kingdom

SAGE Publications India Pvt. Ltd.
M-32 Market
Greater Kailash I
New Delhi 110 048 India

Printed in the United States of America

Library of Congress Cataloging-in-Publication Data

Sigford, Jane L.
   Who said school administration would be fun?: coping with a new emotional and social reality/by Jane L. Sigford.
      p. cm.
   Includes bibliographical references.
   ISBN 0-8039-6659-8 (cloth: acid-free paper).—
ISBN 0-8039-6660-1 (pbk.: acid-free paper)
      1. School administrators—United States—Psychology. 2. School administrators—United States—Social conditions. I. Title.
   LB2831.82.S54 1997
   371.2'00973—dc21   97-33950

98 99 00 01 02 03 10 9 8 7 6 5 4 3 2 1

Editorial Assistant: Kristen L. Gibson
Production Editor: Michele Lingre
Production Assistant: Karen Wiley
Typesetter/Designer: Danielle Dillahunt
Cover Designer: Marcia M. Rosenburg
Print Buyer: Anna Chin

Contents

About the Author iv

Preface v

1. Why Is It So Chilly in the Teachers' Lounge? 1

2. Learning the New Rules of Communication 18

3. Maintaining Control of Your Time 35

4. Developing Your Emotional Teflon 42

5. Maybe You Should Wear a Striped Shirt:
Refereeing Conflict 51

6. Everything You Didn't Know
About Adult Learners 61

7. Looking Into the Mirror of Humor 67

8. Change Is Inevitable, Growth Is Optional 70

9. Power Is Like Love—The More You Give Away,
the More You Have 78

10. Becoming a Self-Assured Administrator 84

References 86

About the Author

Jane L. Sigford, Ed.D., is currently an administrator in the St. Paul Public Schools, St. Paul, Minnesota. Prior to this position, she was a dean of students, an English teacher, special education teacher, learning styles staff development trainer, and reading teacher at a high school in a suburb of Minneapolis. She helped create a drop-in center for divergent learners at the high school.

She has been an adjunct professor for the University of St. Thomas in St. Paul and is currently an adjunct at Hamline University, St. Paul, Minnesota.

She has a B.S. in English from Bermidji State University, Bermidji, Minnesota. Her master's degree in English is from San Diego State University. Her certifications in teaching learning disabled and the emotionally/behaviorally disordered is from the University of St. Thomas, St. Paul, Minnesota. She obtained her doctorate in educational administration from the University of Minnesota, Minneapolis.

She is the proud mother of two adult sons who have contributed greatly to her learning experiences—and her graying hair. Her rural upbringing in Minnesota gave her the challenge of learning to work and play hard, which she still does to this day.

Preface

Genesis of This Book

To paraphrase M. Scott Peck (1978) in *The Road Less Traveled*, "Being a principal is difficult." My position as an administrator in an urban high school combined with the research completed for my dissertation, led me to the realization that administrators are ill-prepared and ill-trained for the socioemotional facets of their jobs.

Administrators and teachers form two of the largest subgroups in the "loosely coupled" hierarchical organization as described by Bolman and Deal (1991). Licensure requirements in most states mandate that administrators have been teachers. There are strong, positive emotional ties to being a teacher. It is a position of respect and awe. There are years of training that must occur before one can be called *teacher*.

However, *principal* or *administrator* does not have the same favorable connotation. Few little children want to grow up to be principal; a principal is that person of power and authority whom students see when they have been sent out of class, when they have been "bad." Teachers even have an odd mixture of respect and resentment toward building principals. After all, the principal is the one who evaluates their job performance and must hold them accountable.

Parents want to work with the school and administration until their own child has specific, unique needs that may cause an adversarial situation. Why would anyone want this job? Why would anyone leave teaching to become an administrator, the job that everyone loves to hate? What kind of person seeks it out and stays? What's more, what does a person have to do to *enjoy* being a principal?

Training for administrators encompasses topics such as personnel management, strategic planning, special education, Management Information Systems (MIS), and scheduling. There are no classes on the socioemotional stages of transition from self-identity as teacher to identity as administrator. The literature does not discuss the stages of change and grief that a person must complete successfully in order to remain and be successful in the position. Therefore, this book came into being.

Purpose

The purpose of this book is to speak to those who are thinking of becoming an administrator in education or business and to support those who are new to the position of management. Even veteran principals/managers may find comfort in the book because it will provide affirmation and recognition of life stages already experienced.

The socioemotional stages experienced by educators are also experienced by persons in business and industry who become part of management in a hierarchical system. Becoming part of another peer group that goes up the ladder of power and influence is a traumatic, important redefinition of self.

This book is unique in that the literature does not deal with the socioemotional stages of professional transitions. We tend to forget that adults, as well as children and adolescents, experience growth stages and transitions. By describing these stages, it is hoped that the transitions become smoother.

For teachers who are thinking of becoming administrators, particularly those who have been nontraditional in that position, such as women and persons of color, this book will describe the experiences of the transition when there may not be other support. For those already in the principalship, the book may validate previous experiences.

Contents of This Book

Overall, this book deals with the inter- and intrapersonal issues that a person must experience when leaving the teaching ranks to become an administrator. At the end of each chapter, there are concrete suggestions to accomplish the task discussed in the chapter.

Chapter 1 discusses the stages of change that translate into the stages of grief and loss. Each stage has emotional work that must be done. Such work is difficult!! Most people are unprepared for the sense of loss that accompanies what is thought of as a promotion.

Chapter 2 discusses the new communication patterns that a person must learn. There are different strategies one must utilize between administrator and teacher, as district spokesperson to staff, and intrapersonally.

Chapter 3 discusses the key issue of time management and the need for flexibility. Thinking that one can manage time in a linear fashion may be self-destructive and doomed to failure.

Especially for nontraditionals in the position, dealing with constant criticism is a learning experience. Most teachers enter the profession because they feel they have something to offer academically. They like people and want people to like them. However, administrators, former teachers by licensure requirements, have to change that expectation because no matter what decision an administrator makes, someone will object. *Chapter 4* discusses what I call the *emotional teflon* needed to deal with this negativity.

Chapter 5 deals with the important skill of resolving conflict. An administrator is seen as the person to mediate personal and professional conflicts. Experience and personal research are the tools most administrators have used to learn strategies in how to be an effective problem solver. There needs to be formal training.

Adult learners are the topic of *Chapter 6.* Until the baby boomer generation, little research had been done on adult learners. Before the current cultural recognition that learning is lifelong, there was the perception that formal learning occurred only in school. Once someone graduated, that part of life was over. The primary population administrators must deal with, however, are adults who are still active learners.

Using humor—the topic of *Chapter 7*—is a vital habit to develop in order to stay content and well-adjusted in the position. Humor is one facet of putting administration into a holistic perspective to deal with the ever-present changes, the topic of *Chapter 8*.

Administration is seen as a position of power. How a principal utilizes and distributes power can be the source of personal success or downfall. How one utilizes power, the subject of *Chapter 9*, must meet the unique culture of each building.

Finally, *Chapter 10* gives a synopsis of the strategies of the first nine chapters to present a self-assured, successful, and happy administrator.

My hope is that the book will be a valuable tool for people who have difficult jobs by providing insight, support, and helpful strategies to make their jobs more affirming and productive.

Why Is It So Chilly in the Teachers' Lounge?

Historical Background

As a new assistant principal, I had my new office, complete with my own direct telephone line, e-mail, and computer. I had access to a secretary, although she was usually overwhelmed with work. I thought I would be able to construct my day in a way that would be an efficient use of my time. Assuming the role of administrator was like visiting a new country; it held new excitements. However, there were many unexpected challenges for which there were no road maps.

My own career journey had progressed through being a classroom teacher, special education teacher, staff development trainer, and administrator. The experiences had been in different districts. My educational preparation and doctoral research had involved discovering the self-determinants of success for the women who were head principals of high schools in Minnesota. In the year 1993-94, there were only 26, a mere 5.6%.

The words of these unique people and my experience led me to the realization that there were many socioemotional aspects of administration that were not part of the formal training required for licensure. Women and persons of color are nontraditional in the position of high school principal. To understand the position as it is today, it is important to reflect on the history of our educational system. To look at administration, we must examine the history of

1

teachers and teaching because administrators come from the teacher pool.

Historically, education has been the domain of men (Lortie, 1975; Shakeshaft, 1987; Tyack & Strober, 1981). The institution reflected the cultural structure present at the time of its inception. Therefore, American education was configured to imitate an early American traditional home in which men were in charge and women nurtured the children. In schools, men were on school boards, held administrative positions, and directed the workings of the schools. As time progressed, teaching became the only respectable occupation open to educated women, even though working outside the home was sharply curtailed (Tyack & Strober, 1981).

Until the late 18th century, all formal teaching was done by men. Women were teachers of small children under 7 years of age, particularly in "dame schools," in small classes in the teachers' homes (Tyack & Strober, 1981). Single women became a ready source of cheap labor to impart middle-class values to students. Teaching as a profession was difficult for married men because salaries were so meager that men often had to have more than one job in order to support their families (Shakeshaft, 1989; Tyack & Strober, 1981). By 1870, when national statistics were available for the first time, women constituted 60% of the teachers; however, most of these were elementary teachers (Tyack & Strober, 1981). There are no statistics about the percentage of women administrators. It was felt, however, that men were meant to be the head of schools as they were meant to be the head of the family.

As the school year lengthened and standards rose, teaching attracted fewer men. If a male was willing to enter a profession that required extensive training, he often sought the more lucrative professions of law and medicine (Tyack & Strober, 1981). Teaching occupied a specialized role in our society in that it required a certain level of educational training and professionalism but did not have the high status or compensation attached to professions such as government, law, medicine, or business (Lortie, 1975).

With the evolution of the graded school, stratification between teachers and administrators and between male and female teachers became even more severe. Since 1905, the majority of teachers have been female, but they have been clustered at the elementary level (Shakeshaft, 1989). Men were seen as more appropriate teachers at the high school level and more appropriate administrators at any level. It was felt that women could not handle the discipline necessary at the upper levels as either teacher or administrator.

Marriage and family were assumed to be a career conflict for women but not for men. It was assumed that working up the career ladder would pose an unusual hardship for women that they would not be willing to endure (Tyack & Strober, 1981). In 1909, Ella Flagg Young became the first female superintendent of the Chicago Public Schools. Her prediction that women would soon take their rightful place as administrators rang hollow. Chicago, like many other American cities, did not appoint another female until 1980, 71 *years* after Young's prediction.

The two "blips" on the graph of involvement in administration by women have been during the Women's Suffrage Movement of the 1920s and the ERA struggles of the 1960s and 1970s. The elementary principalship is the only administrative position in which women have been dominant (Shakeshaft, 1989). It is little known that there were more women in administration in the 1940s (approximately 41%) than in the 1980s (only 20%; Paddock, 1980). Women have never been in the majority as high school principals or superintendents (Shakeshaft, 1987).

In 1972, women constituted 46% of the teachers in secondary schools but only 1% of the senior high principals (Fishel & Pottker, 1974). This statistic was not broken down by assistant and head principal or junior or senior high school. In 1983, women constituted 16% of all principals, elementary and secondary combined. However, there were so few secondary women administrators that the numbers were statistically insignificant. By 1989-90, Jones and Montenegro (1990) found slow overall gains for women. Women constituted 27% of the principals in the nation; principals of secondary schools numbered a meager 12%. However, this statistic is not divided by junior versus senior high, assistant versus head principals, or public versus private/alternative.

The years from 1900 to 1930 were called a golden age for women in administration (Hansot & Tyack, 1981). Women constituted 8% of the principals of secondary schools (Shakeshaft, 1989). After 1928, there was a decline in the number of women in administrative positions, and this did not change until World War II created a shortage of male administrators. Returning soldiers, however, with the advantage of the G.I. Bill and the expectation that women would leave when there were capable men to fill the positions, displaced women once again. In the 1950s, consolidation of many small districts into large districts led to a further decline in the number of female administrators (Shakeshaft, 1989). The Cold War precipitated a backlash against female teachers and administrators because it was felt that men were stronger teachers and leaders and could lead the United States back to its role of world supremacy (Shakeshaft, 1989).

To avoid the draft for the Vietnam War, many men entered the field of education. They were welcomed with open arms, particularly at the elementary level where it was recognized that male teachers were a rarity. However, the influx of male teachers once again led to a scarcity of women administrators despite the Women's Movement of the 1960s and 1970s.

In the 1990s, women and persons of color are still underrepresented in the administrative ranks, which is particularly interesting considering that female teachers outnumber male teachers and administrators come from the teaching ranks. It is a difficult position by nature of its function, but it is even more difficult for those nontraditional to the job, such as women and persons of color. There are few supports either professional or personal for the isolated jobholder. Training institutions concentrate on information as opposed to the socioemotional needs that would enable a person to overcome the entrenched mores of our system.

Teachers Versus Administrators

The bureaucratic, hierarchical structure of schools has created a series of subgroups that vies for scarce resources, attention, and power. Memberships within sub-groups create an identity with their own personal and professional realities. Although being part of a group creates a sense of belonging, it also creates a "we/they" mentality between the groups within the organization.

One of the most powerful struggles within a school is the we/they thinking between teachers and administrators. Teachers perpetuate the separation by lounge talk about administrators. "If only the principal. . . . If only the superintendent. . . ." Teachers criticize administrators because they do not believe that principals remember what it is like in the classroom, and they believe that principals are distanced from students, that they do not follow through on discipline, and that they are out of the building too much.

An administrator, however, has a different framework. She or he must maintain a global perspective. Teachers facilitate the learning for students, which is the ostensible purpose of schools. But to make that happen, administrators must facilitate the smooth interaction of all parts of the school. Transportation must run smoothly. Food service must feed everyone. Custodians must make the environment conducive to learning. Parents must parent, which may sound obvious but does not always happen. Students, the center of the interactions, must learn.

As a teacher, one is part of one of the largest groups in the educational organization. As an administrator, one is part of a very small, powerful, well-scrutinized group. Although there are fewer administrators than teachers, administrators have more power in the bureaucracy. Adapting to that sense of power and difference in job function forces one into a redefinition of purpose and style. To be in charge of all the pieces of the organization is an awesome responsibility. It necessitates the awareness of the importance of each job unit of the school. It mandates looking at a school as through a kaleidoscope, not a telescope, which can only view one thing at a time. In addition, changing identity from teacher to administrator demands an intrapersonal redefinition that training institutions do not address.

The Realization Process

When someone leaves a subgroup, such as teaching, and becomes part of management, such as educational administration, there is a change in the socioemotional reality that must take place. There are procedural stages and coping skills that must be learned in order for the new identity to be adopted successfully. This change in identity occurs whether the person is in education or in business.

The first few weeks on the job are unsettling. It is assumed that a person knows how to be an administrator just by being part of school systems and by having had formal classes. However, that is not true. It is often the case that a person is put in the position and allowed to discover what his or her role and interaction patterns will be. Many people leave teaching to take a type of administrative position before they become a head principal. However, that is not always the case. In my research, I found that 35% of the women went directly to the head principalship from the classroom without the benefit of any mentoring or interning.

Within an administrative office, there is an unspoken assumption that an administrator knows what to do. Other assistant principals, athletic directors, counselors, even secretaries do not feel they have the right to offer advice about how to structure the job for a new administrator. The ethic is that only a direct supervisor may tell someone what to do. It is ironic that the secretaries are probably the best qualified to give pointers and advice.

If someone starts his or her administrative career as an assistant principal, the head principal is responsible for guidance and setting job parameters. It is also true that that person is probably the one who has the least amount of time to provide the guidance and mentoring necessary. What usually happens is that the principal offers overall structure and assumes that the assistant will know how to be self-motivated to define the job. There is a certain amount of belief in the professionalism of the individual that the person will fulfill the job responsibilities. However, administration is like teaching; it is implied that "Here is the job. Now go do it." Other professions, such as medicine or law, have extended internships during which the intern works alongside the teacher for an extended period of time. That does not happen for administrators.

With each job, there is a personal identity and role definition attached. Learning the role takes time. When one changes positions, especially when one changes in the hierarchy of the institution, there are interpersonal and intrapersonal changes that must occur. These changes are rarely discussed. People tend to stumble through them as best they can.

People who have left teaching to become administrators describe the painful separation from their former identity. They realize that their former teacher-friends have become reserved around them. One woman in Minnesota who had come up the ranks in her building to become its administrator still has teachers as close friends. Other women describe the isolation. "There is no one to trust. No one at my level—I can't be friendly with staff." Such words are part of the painful process when one realizes that being "at the top" means that there are few people in the same position, few people from whom to draw support, and few people with similar situations.

Walking into the staff lounge as an administrator is a different experience from walking in as a teacher. The atmosphere feels chilly. Conversations stop or change rapidly. As one woman described it, "The definition [of you] changes as you get up in the organization. I don't sit and have coffee in the lounge anymore." There is not the casual interaction in the hallways that there once was. Conversation in the office rarely crosses the professional boundaries. Administrators and teachers may discuss family and personal interests but on a surface level. There is a hesitancy from teachers in talking to administrators, understandably so because there is a power differential. A principal said, "I know I have people who care about me a lot, including my assistant principals and teachers, but I'm still the boss. There is a limit as to how close you can get."

This separation process from identity as teacher to identity as administrator creates a sense of loss, the same loss that accompanies any major change, even if the change is perceived as positive. Any time there is a change, there is a leaving behind of what is known and familiar. For example, if you are moving to a new city with a promotion, there is still sadness because of leaving friends, family, and the familiar behind. Changing to a new position is the same. There is a sense of excitement and newness but there is a sense of passing time and of losing something that causes one to experience the stages of change.

Stages of Change

In any major change, be it professional or personal, there is a growth process that one must go through to resolve the feelings and redefine the self. This change process is like the grief process as described by Elizabeth Kübler-Ross (1969) in her book, *On Death and Dying*. Kübler-Ross's work with terminally ill patients and families who lost their loved ones led her to describe five stages of grief and loss. These stages are part of any major life change, whether the change is perceived as positive or negative. Leaving teaching to become an administrator is an example of a major change; so too is changing positions from one district to another.

Denial

In a professional change, such as a promotion, the first stage of change lasts about 3 to 6 months. If this change is a promotion, the first stage feels like euphoria. If it is a lateral move or demotion, the person in this stage may feel numb. Kübler-Ross calls this first stage *denial.* In a job promotion, there is a newness and an excitement that makes a person eager to begin the day. There are so many things to learn. There are so many challenges ahead, all of which feel doable at this point. For the purposes of this book, I will discuss only the feelings attached to a promotion of leaving teaching to become an administrator.

The same stages of grief and loss would apply to a demotion or lateral move but would have a less positive slant.

To leave teaching to become an administrator facilitates the discovery of some startling "ahas." One new realization is that the title of *administrator* has more credibility in the eyes of students, parents, and staff. The position itself carries more authority; people assume that if one has the position, one has more knowledge and skills. Even if that is not true, the position itself gives more weight and recognition to what comes out of that office. The words of a teacher and the words of an administrator are not necessarily equal.

The newness of a position with new tasks, new people, even a new office contributes to the denial of the first stage. The newness masks the difficulties and hard parts that lie ahead. In the newness of a position it feels as though any task is doable. The jobholder may not know all the hidden office politics. She or he may not yet have been faced with the work overload. Learning the layout of the office is even fun because it is a change.

The excitement of this new stage can become addictive. It is the stage that people have even in a new interpersonal relationship when everything seems glorious. There is an emotional high that accompanies this excitement that is fun to experience. This newness, however, can become seductive. Sometimes, people get "stuck" in the newness and build up a resistance so they do not have to experience the loss that accompanies this stage. The corollary of the newness is the sadness that a person feels in leaving what is known to go to the unknown. There is a sadness in leaving a known support group and identity in leaving teaching to become an administrator. One is losing identity as teacher and must create a new identity as administrator. That is hard work.

This loss of identity and support is particularly keen for those nontraditionals in the field, such as women and persons of color. In the past, administrative positions in secondary schools have largely been staffed by white men. Although there are far fewer administrators than teachers, there is still a small group of administrative peers for men for camaraderie and support. Because women and persons of color have an even smaller group for support in the administrative ranks, however, the move from teaching to administration is even more isolating. As one woman said, "Now I'm in a glass bowl. People watch carefully. They might misinterpret. There are not a lot of people to talk to."

Another part of the denial stage is that most people, when leaving teaching, still think of themselves as teachers. They do not believe they are any different from when they were teachers. After all, they have had classroom experience and know what it is like. There is a belief that teachers will respect administrative decisions because the administrator was a teacher, and hopefully, a good teacher at that.

It only takes the first unpopular decision for that to change. Conversations suddenly change when the administrator walks by in the hall. Fewer people drop in to the office just to chat. People start making appointments to share their opinion—"just so that you know." There is an emotional distance that was not there previously. The reality of the difficult parts of the job begins to set in.

Anger

Anger, the second stage, surfaces when teachers and administrators have differing opinions. It is a startling realization for a new administrator the first time there is a difference of opinion with teachers. As an administrator, one expects differences of opinion with parents and students but is startled with the number of times it happens with teachers. The surprise comes from the fact that administrators had once been teachers. Because teachers see only such a small piece of the entire operation, they do not have a concept of what other staff members are doing. They assume that everyone works as hard as they do and follows policy and procedures. They do not realize how many times an administrator has to disagree with teachers or to hold them accountable.

Dealing with staff issues is one of the most difficult parts of being an administrator. As a former teacher, one expects teachers to do their jobs and do them well. It is disheartening when that does not occur. That disillusionment causes anger and frustration.

It is particularly frustrating in that staff really does not have an inkling of the turmoil of administration. Because teachers have never been administrators, it is difficult for them to know the hours, the demands, the pressures of the job. It is easy to sit in the lounge and criticize. As former teachers, administrators can almost hear the lounge grousing that occurs.

The anger of the second stage becomes apparent when a person starts blaming other groups, just as they were critical of teachers blaming administrators. It is easier to push some of those bad feelings onto others than it is to recognize that anger was part of the change process itself.

In fact, there is no one faction to blame. Schools are complex systems with complex interactions. What is helpful at this point is to step back and view these feelings as though they are part of a normal *evolution* from teacher to administrator, and not a *result*.

Bargaining

When the rosy feeling of the new job is over and the anger has surfaced, it is time to progress to the third stage: *bargaining*. One begins to develop coping strategies and methods of improving the position. One example is that administrators try to work on increasing communication. No school will ever say that there is enough communication.

A strategy for one principal was to improve her listening. "I cannot overemphasize the importance of listening. Listening is as important as politics and helps people along." Another strategy was to "have key leaders from the building . . . work hard at having people confront issues, not talk behind people's backs."

Another principal had a "lot of brainstorming and sharing. It sometimes gets into shouting and arguing with each other but we work it out." One principal described it as "various groups . . . all have parts of a puzzle to look at. I try to get various groups to have ownership but not be bogged down."

All those strategies are excellent in fostering communication and empowering staff members. Those strategies are some of the external remedies necessary to build a new internal definition of self. No matter how someone defines the issues within a school and tries to remedy them, the bargaining becomes part of a process that must be completed for a new self-identity to be realized.

Depression

The fourth stage, *depression,* may be disguised as frustration, exhaustion, and stress. It can be characterized by self-doubt. It is at this point that some administrators think about leaving to return to teaching, to move to a new district, or to pursue a career in other areas, such as curriculum, college teaching, or a superintendency. The faulty assumption is that any of those positions would be less stressful. Some people leave during this stage because it is so hard. It does not feel good. Some people want to feel the euphoria of the newness of Stage one all over again. Unfortunately, because of the stages of change, the stage of depression will recur in the next new position as well.

Depression is common, especially toward the end of the second year. The honeymoon is over. Bargaining did not work, and the job seems difficult. It is important to realize that this stage is necessary and unavoidable. For some people, it is short-lived and barely recognizable, but it does occur.

Acceptance

The final stage, *acceptance,* becomes apparent when one realizes a feeling of pride and satisfaction over an administrative accomplishment. There is a feeling of satisfaction in making a difference in the lives of students, of making a change, of creating something new. Acceptance occurs when the disagreements with staff, parents, and students no longer feel personal. It is as though there is a Plexiglas shield around the body so that one can see and deal with issues, but they do not cause personal damage. Certainly, there will always be discouraging days, but the problems do not seem unsolvable. There is an acceptance that comes when there is a pattern of repeat problems. "Oh, I've done this before. I can handle this." It is like making the master schedule for the second time. The first time through feels fragmented, complex, and intimidating. The second time, one knows what to expect, so it is no longer frightening. By the third time, one can even pre-empt some of the problems.

The job is difficult. Not everyone will agree with what an administrator does. In fact, if no one disagrees, a person wonders if there is something wrong. There is a milestone of acceptance when an administrator can walk into the teachers' lounge and describe it as "removed," not chilly. Administrators are removed from teachers as part of their job. That is part of the acceptance of the position.

The Task of Each Stage

Each stage of change has a purpose and a lesson that must be learned for the process to continue. Sometimes, people get stuck in a stage. They may create situations in which they repeat a stage over and over rather than completing the process. For example, when a person accepts a new job, there is a euphoria that is exhilarating to experience. When some of the struggles of the new job begin to set in, however, some people may actually change jobs rather than feel the pain. If someone constantly avoids the pain, they end up recreating the same situation over and over. They move from job to job or district to district to feel the excitement rather than completing the process of change.

Others recreate job situations in which they are angry about how hard they work in comparison to other people. When their job starts going better, they will create a situation so they can feel angry once more. They are recognizable by their language because they are always blaming someone else for what is happening. They blame teachers, superintendents, parents, school boards, and students. They seem to hate their job.

Anger is like love in that it produces endorphins in the body. Some people become addicted to that physical feeling and consistently recreate situations that cause them to feel anger. They become "anger junkies."

Others may get stuck in the bargaining by constantly trying to reconcile factions. They never get to the point of self-assurance and realize that what they do is not going to be acceptable to all people. They believe to a fault that if they work harder and smarter, then all will be well. Such thinking is destructive because it never looks at the responsibilities that others have in any relationship.

Others are depressed. They feel the world, their friends, their training, and even life in general has failed them. They wallow in their own self-pity and blame everyone else for their discomfort. If something starts going well, they will put a negative slant on it. It will still never be good enough.

The process of change is not linear, nor is it gradual. It is more like a roller-coaster ride with uneven ups and downs. The process can happen more than once. In reality, the five stages appear and reappear whenever a person experiences a major life change. It can happen when a person changes jobs, districts, schools, and it can happen in any personal change, such as marriage, divorce, children leaving home, or a broken leg.

The intensity of each stage will vary with the degree of personal involvement in the event. For example, the stages may be very pronounced if one is strongly attached to a job, a community, or a staff. Some people will stay in a position for many years to avoid going through the change process.

For personal major changes, the process takes 6 months to 2 years. The ability to label the stages and talk about them makes the process less frightening. One stage may take longer than another. Or a person may go through a stage and then slide back into a previous stage. The return trip, however, is seldom as long as the first time if you have done the incumbent work of each stage. The process is not smooth; in fact, it is messy. It is a necessary part of the socioemotional development for any change.

The Work of Each Stage

Each stage has tasks that must be successfully accomplished. The work of the first stage, *denial,* is to help one separate and redefine. It is the stage to cut loose from those things that are no longer necessary. It is part of letting go. It is the beginning of taking what was learned from the previous experiences to integrate with the new.

Hanging on to the label of teacher is part of denial. Administrators are still teachers but in a very different sense. The instruction is more likely to be procedural or process learning, particularly because administrators are working with adult learners who have different needs from those of children.

Administrators are more likely to teach one-on-one or in small groups. Teacher evaluations are a good example. Conferencing with a teacher to improve instruction is a type of teaching. Although it is vastly different from standing in front of a classroom of 25 teenagers, it is equally powerful. That teacher will go to his or her classroom and change methodology for the 150 students she or he sees each day. Although it is harder to assess the effect of what an administrator teaches because it is siphoned through the teachers, the instruction is no less valuable than direct classroom instruction. In fact, it can be more powerful because it affects so many more students.

The work of the second stage, *anger,* is to facilitate the separation from the former position to the present one. People have a tendency to cling to old ideas unless there is a good reason to let go. One of the easiest ways to let go is to get angry. Leaving something behind is painful, and it can make someone either sad or angry. Unaware people are more likely to choose the anger because it feels stronger than the sadness. It is necessary, however, to realize that anger is a cover-up emotion, often masking fear or sadness.

An example of the purpose of anger is illustrated by a story I tell seniors in high school when they come to me depressed and angry in the spring of the year. I tell them that being a senior is the hardest year of their school lives. So many people have told them that being a senior is wonderful, but many students experience a roller-coaster year. There are so many "lasts" during this time. The last basketball game. The last pep fest. The last dance. Students have not lived long enough to realize there are many "firsts" just waiting. The pain is particularly prevalent around prom time. So many students stay with their boyfriend/girlfriend until prom is over. Then they break up.

These stages are appropriate pieces of the change process. Students get angry with their friends and significant others because it feels stronger and less vulnerable than feeling sad. Being sad feels helpless and weak. Therefore, students have a tendency to use anger to help them make the separations and say good-bye. Adults use the same mechanisms when they make a major life change. Anger can be helpful to make us move on as long as the anger does not become a crutch, and recognizing anger for its purpose helps us leave it behind with the fear and sense of sadness.

The task of the third stage, *bargaining,* is to begin fusing denial and anger to refocus on the future. The work of the first two stages is to say good-bye to the past. Bargaining provides a bridge to the work of the future. It is the beginning of bringing together the experiences from teaching and what is being learned about administration. It is this fusion that is the prelude to the new self-identity. Bargaining is a stage when new management skills are learned. It is at this time that administrators go beyond the training that they had in college and begin looking for new avenues to do a better job. This part of the cycle when the rollercoaster is heading back up feels much better than the anger.

The fourth stage, *depression*, is necessary for the final letting go and the resultant growth that can then occur. If someone cannot keep moving forward, it is at this stage that he or she leaves to take another position, return to teaching, or move to a central office position. This stage often occurs around the end of the second year of administration.

In depression, the rollercoaster has taken a downturn, which does not feel good. The person has progressed through the other stages with the euphoria, the anger, has begun to try new things again, but still not everything works as well as one would like. Teachers, parents, and students are still unhappy sometimes. The job still feels overwhelming. Usually, a person has been out of the classroom long enough that that becomes romanticized in the mind. One has a tendency to forget the mounds of papers to correct. One forgets the pressures of three (or more) daily preparations. It sounds like fun to be in charge of a classroom in which things happen and kids learn. This is the final and crucial stage before one can move on to a new socioemotional reality.

The final upturn of the ride comes with *acceptance*, occurring around the third year in the position. It takes that long for ideas to gel, for programs that were set in motion to begin taking effect, and for a person to change his or her self-perception. By the end of the third year, however, one can begin to see the sprouts of change. About this time, one realizes that going back to teaching is not an option. In fact, there are times when one realizes that one has more excitement and more challenges as an administrator. People seldom leave administration to return to a mainstream classroom. Some may go on to teach at the college level, but that has different rewards and fewer constraints than does teaching in a K-12 setting. Acceptance feels good.

Not only do humans experience the change process, systems do, too. The change process for humans takes 6 months to 2 years. For systems change, as in a building, it may take 5 to 7 years for an effort to become part of the culture. People are going through the stages of change and so are systems. The interplay and interaction make up the dynamic, interesting part of schools. Understanding the process greatly helps the redefinition and feelings of success.

We never learn about these emotional stages when we are in graduate school. Professors tend to ignore discussing the socioemotional parts of the job. They may not even know about these stages because most professors have gone through school and directly into higher education.

Not only do college courses neglect these stages, but by the very nature of schools, we as administrators are so isolated from our small peer group that we have little or no opportunity to discuss such topics. It is through the recognition and acceptance of these stages, however, that administrators become successfully socialized to their position.

No one said change would be easy. The roller-coaster effect is painful, but after every downturn there is an upturn, and the contrast between the hills and valleys diminishes with each succeeding stage. The important part of the process is to recognize the work that must be done. There are no shortcuts. But there are many rewards.

Suggestions for How to Deal With the Change Process

1. To deal with change successfully, one must recognize that there are stages. Naming and describing the stages makes them less frightening. Information is the first step to being able to manage and predict. Part of knowing the stages is to recognize that there will be backsliding between them, but the return slip is shorter than the first time if the work inherent to the stage has been accomplished.

2. Learn to forgive if there is a return to a previous stage. Just like dieting, if there is a slip, do not give up. Start again tomorrow.

3. Experience the stages, do not withdraw from them. They are necessary components of the internal change process. To avoid them means that they will recur in a different fashion and will have to be dealt with anyway. People have a tendency to avoid that which is painful. Avoidance, however, is merely a short-term remedy to a long-term problem. Like the seniors in high school, it is necessary to go through the stages in order to go on to something better.

4. Look forward to the next stage. To look backward continually means that one will miss the scenery ahead.

5. Practice proactivity. Record this journey in some way, such as in a journal. Some people use a drawing journal. Others feel comfortable recording their thoughts on tape. It is helpful to have some hard-copy account to use as an instrument of reflection; it helps put the jigsaw pieces into the whole puzzle. Save these thoughts to re-read in a few months. The gift of time and distance helps put the journey into a powerful perspective that provides many unexpected insights.

6. Find someone at a similar professional stage. Structure time together to discuss experiences. Free time is a luxury, but reflection and support are necessary to experience and use the stages for proper development. Join a principals' organization to find someone. Join Phi Delta Kappa. Start a study group within your district.

7. Do something apart from education as a way to keep a perspective. It is too easy to become single-focused. It is most important not to get to that point. Find several things that transport the mind and body away from education. Read "garbage" novels. Run. See plays. Walk in the woods. Fish. Watch the crackling fire in the fireplace. Such outlets are not only escapes but also avenues for the brain to rest and come back refreshed.

8. Recognize that change is certain; growth is optional. Life will change and people will change. One can either be an active participant in charge of the process by being aware of it, or one can be controlled *by* it. Most people prefer being in charge.

2

Learning the New Rules of Communication

Becoming an administrator necessitates a change in communication patterns. There are distinct communication groups—building administrators, teachers, noncertified staff, and district office—each with its own rules. The communication between and within a group depends on a person's peer group. The amount of perceived power of the group and the number of members within the group help shape communication styles. When someone changes peer groups, particularly moving up the hierarchy from teacher to administrator, a new set of communication patterns is necessary.

Communication Between Groups

According to the work of David Tyack and Myra Strober (1981), American schools were created as a reflection of the family system that was in practice at the time. The father, head of the family, was in charge. Power and authority rested in the position and were dispersed at the whim and beneficence, or lack thereof, of the person. There was a hierarchy: father, father and mother, and children. Power, traveling down, diminished on the lower rungs of the hierarchy.

The same hierarchy is replicated in our school system. There is the macro system of the district and the micro system within a building. At the macro level, the superintendent is in the seat of authority. At the micro level, the head principal is in charge, with power filtering through assistant principals. At a micro micro level, teachers are in charge of their classrooms, and students have less power and control. The entire structure is like a hologram. Each piece looks like the whole.

The hierarchical and segmented structure of our educational system has created a series of in-groups and out-groups. The different subgroups are denoted by their different bargaining units. Paraprofessionals, custodians, food-service workers, teachers, clerical staff, administrators, superintendent, and school board constitute some of the subgroups. When groups are in competition with one another for differences in pay, an automatic barrier in communication and trust is created. In our school culture, the person who makes the most money has the most power and prestige. This is true at a macro and micro level. Therefore, communication becomes inhibited due to the unequal resources.

Communication patterns between groups reflect these differences. Within a group, communication occurs relatively equally between peers. Communication and socialization are more likely to be open and honest than between groups.

Communication either down or up the hierarchy, however, is less likely to be completely open. Going down the ladder of prestige, as from teacher to custodian, administrator to teacher, communication is likely to be in the form of directive. Teachers may tell custodians, "Please clean my room every day, not every other." Administrators tell teachers what to do. "We ask that teachers stand outside their door between classes." Superintendents will tell principals that they must submit budget requests by April 1. Personal communication around areas, such as family, hobbies, interests, is relatively limited. It may happen if two people discover a commonality, such as fishing, but even then may be superficial.

Likewise, if communication goes up the structure, it is likely to be guarded because of the power differential. It is often requesting something—information, money, or time. People lower in the hierarchy do not want to make themselves vulnerable. Teachers are not likely to be completely honest with their principals about their fears of professional inadequacy. Principals are not likely to be completely open with the superintendent about everything that occurs within a building for fear of being seen as incompetent. Each person decides just how open to be with his or her superior.

Communication between groups in schools is a common focus of improvement in almost any school. Those in groups further down in the hierarchy would say that they never know what is going on. Teachers would say that directives come down from the top, but there is little real communication with true sharing of ideas. Administrators talk *at* them, but do not listen or share ideas. The format of schools themselves creates this communication bottleneck.

Exacerbating the problem is the compartmentalized daily task of teaching. Elementary teachers spend their day in their classrooms with "their" classes. They often socialize professionally and personally along grade level lines. Fifth grade teachers may meet and share ideas. First grade teachers may plan parties together.

High school teachers spend their day teaching their 150 students in *their* room. They often socialize along departmental lines. Meetings are held for departments. Math teachers will meet to decide how to do sectioning, for example. Math teachers seldom meet with art teachers, even on a social level.

Communication Within a Group

Because of the pyramidal structure of schools, there is less opportunity for communication among peers as one goes up the ladder. Teachers form the largest of the subgroups, creating more possibilities for a sense of fraternity.

There are far fewer administrators than teachers. Therefore, when one leaves the ranks of teacher to become an administrator, the patterns of communication change drastically in the sheer number of opportunities to interact with peers. It becomes very lonely. As one principal described it, "There are people I do things with but there is no one in town I'm really close to." It is not easy. Another principal said: "My mentor told me not to befriend any teachers because there will come a time when you will have to go counter to their wishes" (Sigford, 1995).

Changes

One of the biggest losses people feel when they become part of the administrative team is the change in friendships with teachers who were former peers but are now subordinates. New ground rules must be established as to what are appropriate topics of conversation and what are not. Teachers often share complaints about administration. When one is promoted within the system, however, it is no longer possible to take part. Another difficulty arises from the fact that, as an administrator, one is privy to confidential information. Now when teacher-friends have complaints and concerns, the new administrator must remain silent. Teachers may resent the fact that communication patterns have changed. They may resent the fact that an administrator knows more and cannot or will not share information. Some friendships may not survive the change in position because of the change in the power differential. It takes a true friend to be able to understand the change in boundaries and authority.

Even casual friendships change when a person becomes an administrator, especially if the promotion occurs within the same system. For example, in one of my buildings, we had a book club composed of teachers. When I became an administrator, I wondered if I could continue. I lasted for a few months until it became too uncomfortable. Conversations at book club would be about the book but invariably the conversation strayed to talk about school. Teachers would ask me questions about policy. Sometimes, they would be talking about issues that I could not discuss, including disparaging comments about administration. Much of it was meant as venting but it still was uncomfortable. I gradually had to phase out, partly because of increased evening commitments and later because I moved to a new district.

With this new position in the power hierarchy, it is easier to maintain friendships with teacher-friends if one changes districts. Then the boundaries between professional and personal can stay intact. Teachers can discuss administrators without the new administrator having a conflict of interest. The new administrator can reflect on teachers without teachers taking it personally.

As one principal described it, "When the rest of my colleagues as teachers were developing social relationships and friendship teams, I was already a principal so that those networks and teams are more limited" (Sigford, 1995).

Communication About *The District*

In the macro system, administrators in the buildings are the "middle persons" within a district who must be responsible for delivering district information and edicts. Principals relay information from Central Office. It is expected that principals will support Central Office publicly, even if they disagree personally.

The same system is true in the micro system of the building. Assistant principals are expected to support the decision of the principal publicly, even if they disagree personally. This expectation is like that of the early American family. Both parents present the same unified front to the children, even if the parents disagree between themselves.

Each professional owes a certain respect and allegiance to the institution that pays his or her salary. Yet each person owes the same respect to his or her personal values. If there is a conflict between the two, the professional must decide how to deal with it.

One choice is to work for a different district. Another is to agree with the district, no matter what. Another choice is to rebel and be prepared for the consequences. Another is to practice "creative insubordination." For example, if there is a district decision to become involved in a certain staff development project districtwide and the principal knows that this is not valuable or is inappropriately timed, the principal may choose to be the last on the list of schools to implement it. By the time the district gets around to it, the movement may have passed. Although such a practice is passive-aggressive, it may be necessary for survival. A person can agree with the essence of the policy but disagree privately or subtly in practice by delaying action or practicing minimal compliance.

Another pattern is that it may be necessary to tell only half the story. Sometimes, teachers do not need or want to know the whole story. It is wise to keep teachers informed about upcoming events that will affect them. Although many teachers want information, they do not want to be overloaded with useless knowledge. They want administrators to take care of the politics and policies so they can do what they do best—teach. They want a good administrator to clear the way for that to happen. Therefore, if teachers do not need to know the whole story, then tell only the parts they need to know when they need to know them.

Within the Role of Administrator

One part of the role of administrator includes being what I call a "supra-parent." Administration is communication. Some of it is written, although most of the day is spent in interactions with people. Many people want to tell the principal something, ask advice, or just connect. Others want feedback or help with a problem. This supra-parent role, like the "father" of the hierarchical system of American schools, puts administrators in the role of Grand Communicator of the building. Staff, students, and parents look to the administration as the expert, the "bottom line," the problem solver, and sometimes, the priest/priestess. It is a difficult role to fill, one for which we receive little advance training.

As an assistant principal, I watched the demands placed on the head principal. Everyone wanted to have her attention and ear. They needed information from her. Furthermore, they wanted to keep her apprised of what was happening in the building.

I watched a guidance counselor interact with our principal. I watched as he told her every detail about the setup for schoolwide testing. I knew that she did not need to know each nuance of the setup because she trusted him to act professionally and accomplish the task. What she needed to know was if there was something he needed from her. He had a tendency to spend 15 minutes telling her every detail when he could have spent only 5 minutes and then ask his questions about a logistics issue.

What I realized at that point was that I had a tendency to talk to her and other principals in "sound bytes." I knew that I could give her the bottom line and she would ask probing questions if she needed more information. I later shared my strategy with her. She laughed and asked if I would share that with other people, especially with the guidance counselor. Because of his need for connection and approval, he wanted to make certain that the principal had all the appropriate information. What he did not understand is that her job as principal assumed she had the large overview. What she needed was the bottom line; what he needed, however, was the approval of the "supra-parent."

His interchange with her took more than 15 minutes. In a building with 2,000 students, 120 teachers and staff, plus custodians, food service, parents and families of all the students, the community interactions, and district responsibilities, there are not enough 15-minute blocks of time to go around. Even if most interactions take 5-7 minutes, a principal would have time for 78 single interactions throughout a school day, during school hours. If each interaction took 15 minutes, she or he would have time for only 26—without any time for lunch. As we know, meetings, parent conferences, and other problems may take an hour or more. It is no wonder that most administrators carry on more than one conversation at a time. It is not unusual to see an administrator on the telephone and writing a message about another issue at the same time, and two people waiting in line to talk. There is not enough time in the day for all the interactions that people would like.

Another part of the Grand Communicator role is to realize that teachers have a tendency to repeat themselves to a fault. It is as though they are in the classroom and want to make certain that everyone has the information. Unfortunately, when they repeat everything three times, students and administrators alike tune out after the first time. It is difficult as an administrator to pay close attention to the details when time is short and what is really crucial are the facts and the bottom line.

Few people realize the sheer number of interactions an administrator has throughout the day. There is always a stack of phone messages to return, items clipped to the door that need a response, and personal interactions.

It is necessary to learn to listen for the real message. As an administrator, one realizes that the job consists of communication skills of being responsive, being effective at giving information, and, particularly, being a good listener, which means hearing the message that may be hidden in the spoken words. For example, if a teacher comes to discuss how "some" teachers are not doing their job (standing in the hall between classes), it may take time and knowledge of the staff to know that the real issue is that his next-door teaching neighbor, whom he does not like, is not standing in the hall. This teacher wants the administrator to reprimand the other teacher.

Granted, the superficial message of getting teachers to stand in the hall is valuable. If the administrator had heard only that part, the real issue would not have been addressed. When the administrator realizes that the real issue is to get back at another staff member, then the administrator can make an intelligent choice of how to deal with the issue. The actions change if the real message is retaliation rather than equal distribution of the workload. To get at the real issue, an administrator must do more than hear. She or he must *listen actively* to the words, the intent, the body language, and the nuances. Actual words are a small part of a communication.

Much of what an administrator does is resolving issues. **Being able to listen, rephrase, and reframe is important to the permanent resolution.** (There is more on this skill in Chapter 5, on conflict.)

Part of being a good listener is separating the issue from the presenter. For example, some teachers may have an abrupt, gruff manner. When asked to patrol the halls before a vacation, a teacher may fire back, "It's not my job." It is up to the administrator to help that person understand the big picture of how everyone must help on intense days. This same abrupt teacher may be very thorough and insightful in the classroom. Therefore, it is necessary to divorce the communication style from the person.

Administrators are victims of a constant barrage of negative comments, complaints, and interactions. One can hear the comment in the staff lounge, "That's why they [administrators] make the big bucks." That is partly true. It is the task of the administrators to be responsive to problems. The staff, community, and students go to administrators as a last resort, often when they have been dissatisfied with communication from a person lower in the hierarchy. Often, the person has been through more than one person and received personally dissatisfying information. By the time the person comes to an administrator, he or she is tired of repeating the story, is angry, and frustrated. **It is up to the administrator to listen beyond anger and resolve the issue.**

It is doubly important at this juncture to listen to the real issue. When a person is frustrated or upset, the surface emotions are what come out first. The real emotions and concerns come out after talking for a while. To listen beyond the words and to take the time to get to the heart of the problem requires energy, time, heart, and empathy. After listening to the issue, it may be necessary to reframe. For example, an angry parent on the telephone begins by expressing anger about how the teacher has not communicated with the parents on a regular basis when the student was not doing well in class. After some time spent in clarifying what happened, it is often the case that the parent is, in fact, angry with the child but is displacing that anger onto the school and teacher. It takes time to listen beyond the anger and refocus on the real issue of what the student is doing.

Listening beyond expressed anger is often difficult as an administraotr, however, because so much of the communication an administrator hears is either angry or frustrated. Administrators hear it from students, parents, teachers, community members, the district office, and custodians. Some people feel a certain impunity in "dumping" on administrators because administrators cannot "dump" back. Teachers can say some harsh things to principals but principals must be careful about what to say in return. Because of the evaluative position of administration and the laws regarding employee practices, an administrator often has to listen intently, respond, but not share a true opinion.

For example, I had an exchange one day with a probationary teacher who was inappropriate with students. The teacher wanted me to suspend a student when the power struggle had been initiated and precipitated by the teacher. I would not do it. The teacher accused me of not doing my job. If I had retorted that he was not doing his job, the comment would become evaluative and proscribed by policy and laws regarding teacher tenure. I had to listen to the teacher but understand that his lack of experience and understanding did not precipitate a tirade on my part. I was the professional and had to act like it. Granted, I wanted to vent at him the same way he vented at me, but I had to understand that his anger came from lack of experience and understanding, which is what I tried to share with him.

People often think that administrators are at the top of the hierarchy, but when it comes to negativity, the hierarchy is inverted. Administrators then become the bottom of a very large pile. Many people feel they can say anything they want to an administrator and the administrator must take it. To a degree that is true. Administrators are the first to hear if something is wrong and one of the last to hear if something is good. Communications from teachers, students, and parents will come to the administration quickly if it is about something negative. The positive statements do not flow as freely and are more dispersed to the staff.

Communication Distancing

It is difficult to withstand constant negativity and not take it personally. Administrators need to establish a pattern that I call *communication distancing* in order to survive. To do this, one must know one's self very well and must also be able to separate the message from the message giver.

Part One: When to Tell the Whole Truth

Part one of the distancing is to know when to relay the whole truth and when to tell a half-truth. An administrator must learn to be honest—with protection. It is important that the principal relay information from the superintendent and school board. Yet there are times when the principal may not tell the whole truth. There are times when parents come to talk to the principal. For example, a parent has a concern that his or her child is not learning in the social studies class. Parents do not see homework. The child complains that he or she has never gotten assignments turned back. But at progress report time, the child has a failing grade. The parents complain to the principal. What the parents do not and cannot know is that the principal is working on a corrective action plan for that teacher because the teacher is not doing the job correctly. The principal, however, has to develop the communication skills of listening to the parents and letting them know that there is action being taken without defaming the teacher. Here the administrator must be honest with the parents, but not totally so.

Part Two: Knowing When Anger Is Not Really Anger

Part two of communication distancing involves knowing when anger that is directed at an administrator is really a part of the denial stage of the grief process. By the time someone gets to an administrator, they are often angry. A parent comes to your office irate that his daughter has not received total cooperation with her 504 plan, a federal program designed to help students who have disabilities. He has been frustrated because he is not getting the support he felt necessary from teachers and counselors. By the time he gets to the administrator, he has already experienced several layers of the school and has not gotten what he perceives as necessary.

At this point, it may be an effective strategy to let him vent, knowing that it is not personal. The next step is to ask him what he would like, assuring him that both school and family want what is best for his daughter. The third step is to formulate an action plan. The fourth step is to plan a time to come back to revisit how things are going, either by telephone or in person. The follow-up is crucial. It delivers the message that the school is serious and will not drop the issue as soon as the parent leaves the room.

This example is used because this parent's anger, like many others, may be symptomatic that this parent is stuck in a stage of the grief/change process discussed in Chapter 1. When any child is born, parents have dreams and ideals of what this child will be. Those children seldom materialize. Parents have to go through the stages of grief, particularly in the case of disabilities or handicaps. If the parent has not completed the process, she or he will continually blame the school, society, the ex-wife or ex-husband, or any other scapegoat. Understanding that the venting of anger onto the school is part of the denial process makes it easier to withstand someone yelling at you in the office. It also helps to honor the stage of grief within the parent. It may point the way to suggesting other resources and support groups to the parent. It may be a way to refer for counseling.

Part Three: Maintaining Distant Relationships in a Building

Part three of distancing is knowing how to maintain respectful, yet distant, relationships in a building. It is very difficult to be friends with people whom one has to supervise and evaluate. As a teacher, one had the opportunity to have a friendship with many teachers. As one of a very small team of administrators, one may or may not find a comrade. It may be that one works hard, does what is expected, and finds supportive relationships outside the building and maybe outside the profession.

Some principals who are in isolated areas said they maintained contacts with friends who live in a different community. One said that she used to "call my friends, cry, and have a big phone bill" (Sigford, 1995).

Generally, it is not a good idea to become a close personal friend with someone within the building. The power and information differential causes too many awkward situations. There are things that teachers cannot know. Anyone who has worked in a school knows the rapid gossip network within a staff. It is an oxymoron to share a secret. Therefore, if an administrator wants to protect privacy, she or he cannot confide in anyone because of the temptation the other person has to tell just one person, share one little piece.

It is normal to discuss students and staff with others in our building. Information about people is a rapidly exchanged commodity. Even if an administrator shares impressions or ideas, those thoughts have a market value in the lounge. Everyone wants to know about what the administrators think and do. What they do has an influence on the entire school. Therefore, it is important that an administrator maintain a certain self-protective distance from persons in the building.

Because the position of administrator is lonely and there are few peers, administrators tend to gravitate toward counselors as possible sympathetic ears. Part of the reason is that administrators and counselors are in close working proximity. Counselors are in a unique position in a building by being on the teachers' contract but having an extended yearly contract more like that of an administrator. Counselors often have a more global perspective on the workings of a school than do teachers. They have to deal with the whole school, as does an administrator. Their hours and daily demands from teachers are different, which puts them on the fringe of the teachers' in-groups.

Teachers often see counselors as neither teacher nor administrator. In small systems, a counselor may even fill in for an administrator when an administrator is out of the building. Counselors are victims of the we/they mentality of teachers' lounges, as are administrators, because teachers can blame counselors for classes that are too large when new students are placed in them.

Therefore, counselors and administrators often find themselves more aligned physically and professionally than do administrators and teachers. Yet a friendship with a counselor is open to criticism. An administrator is still in an evaluative position over a counselor. If an administrator becomes friends with a counselor, it may be awkward for the administrator to share complaints about the counselor by a parent or a faculty member with that person. The counselor may be compromised because teachers or other counselors can be critical of possible plush assignments by an administrator.

When it comes to power and the information network, however, counselors are more aligned with teachers than are administrators. They are more welcome in the teachers' lounge than are administrators. Therefore, it is important to develop a good working relationship with counselors but equally important to maintain a communication distance from them.

Part Four: Distance Within the Administrative Ranks

Part four deals with the communication distance one experiences within the administrative ranks. Everyone needs someone to talk to; administrators are no different. Administrators are most secure in confiding with other administrators. That relationship may also be problematic. If the administrative team is not cohesive, it is difficult to share with people who may be competitive on their way to the top. It may be difficult to find someone on a small team who thinks the same way as you do.

One principal used MASSP, Minnesota Association of Secondary School Principals, to develop a support network. Another said: "The men have their fishing. We [women administrators] get together and talk. I get recharged because I have professional friends" (Sigford, 1995).

Confiding in administrative superiors is fraught with difficulty. For an assistant principal, it can be problematic to be completely open with the principal. Principals may be reserved in what they share with superintendents, although in small districts, principals may confide in superintendents as the only peers within the system. Communications are guarded, however, because of the power differential. There remains a distance. Truly open communication rarely goes up the power ladder. A principal is quoted as having said, "Now it's hard to have friends at my own level. There is only 'one of me' at my level. This professional distance is hard because there are few women to relate to" (Sigford, 1995).

Because the power differential is so far removed, it is not surprising that administrators often confide in their head secretaries. The administrator feels safe in sharing because there is a wide gap between the level of responsibilities for principal and secretary. Yet the secretary sees the school through a wide-angle lens unlike the narrow focus of teachers. The secretary is there as a watchdog and as helpmate for the principal. She or he is in a prime position to feed the administrator much powerful information about the building. There is a certain protective feeling a good secretary has for an administrator. The secretary knows many personal details about the administrators because she or he fields phone calls, visitors, and appointments. An administrator often shares personal feelings because of the unique relationship.

However, it is the rare secretary who feels free to reciprocate the confidences. Secretaries are selective in what personal information they share with the principal. The differential is evident in the fact that many head principals do not have more than a surface knowledge of the personal lives of their secretaries. Secretaries see what happens to the administrators but the opposite is seldom true.

In the days of only male principals, the head custodian was sometimes the same type of safety valve as the head secretary. The old boiler room was a place for the principal to have a cigarette, tell a few stories, and relax. The power differential continued. A custodian could not say the same things to a principal as the principal could say to the custodian.

Part Five: Emotional Detachment

Part five of the distancing process deals with the concept that administrators are expected to be emotionally detached from information. They are expected to be steadfast, nonemotional, concerned, and even-tempered. When angry, they are expected to control their temper. When sad, they are expected to control their tears. In fact, if an administrator is too demonstrative, confidence in him or her decreases.

If there is tension, anger, sadness, or other feelings in the building, the whole building is fine if the administrator is stoic and strong. If, however, the administrator is shaky, then the whole building is shaky. As in a family, if the head of the family is OK, then the rest of the family is also.

Unfortunately, the demonstration of feelings has been misinterpreted culturally as being weak or ineffectual. It is not true that the demonstration of sadness, joy, anger, or happiness makes one less effective as an administrator. Our white male model, however, has left us this ethos. Administrators are to be involved but detached, which is a difficult road to walk. If a person—particularly a female—shows emotion, she or he is viewed with suspicion. It is difficult to show emotion and have a staff take one seriously. It is as if the demonstration of anger or tears makes one incapable and too unstable to do the job well.

Recognition of this hidden standard is difficult for women. Culturally, American women have been trained to be the emotions for a relationship and/or family. Women administrators may be a vital force in changing the traditionally stoic image. The ability to display feelings appropriately may be humanizing for a building. Schools are institutions whose clients are people. It is valuable to teach our children and staff alike that the appropriate expression of feelings is healthy.

The same is true for persons of other cultures. Open displays of affection and anger by males and females are appropriate in many cultures. It is my hope that new administrators, particularly women and persons of color, will be judged by the competence of their actions and not by their surface stoicism. Many women I interviewed for my dissertation found it difficult to curb their normal emotional responses to events. They had to keep their feelings to a very few trusted friends or spouses and demonstrate them behind closed doors. "You can't say what you'd like to say."

Even with her spouse as support-person, one woman said, "Funny, because I never talk about school with him because he gets bored. But he's always there." Women learn to close their door and emote in private, maintaining a public persona of control. For women and persons of different cultures who have been allowed to express feelings, it is difficult to come to a middle ground of expressing feelings from a detached perspective.

Suggestions for Establishing Communication Patterns

1. The only true secret is one not shared with another. If something is truly a secret, then do not tell anyone.

2. Develop peers, outside your building, who can act as sounding boards and confidantes. Such people may be found in professional organizations or as administrators in other buildings within the district or in similar positions in different systems.

3. It is necessary to find a safe place within the building where you can regroup. This may be a place to which you can escape for a few minutes, such as the office of a support person (e.g., the office of the

gifted/talented coordinator), the kitchen, or the custodian's work-room.

4. Mentally rehearse a previous difficult conversation as though it were being seen through a video camera. What would the lens see?

Each time you get into a conversation that is difficult, call back that camera. Look at the situation as though you are looking through that detached machine, instead of through your emotions. What would have been different? Was it too emotional? Or were the emotions appropriate and necessary? Looking through a nonemotional lens helps put a conversation into a different context.

5. Take time. It is important to take time to think and look at an issue from a wide lens perspective. If a teacher presents an issue, listen to the details, take notes, and then take 24 hours to think it over, if possible. It is not necessary to make a decision or give a response immediately. In fact, sometimes by waiting a day, the issue will take care of itself. Do not stall just to avoid a difficult issue, but use time as an ally and possibly seek another opinion.

6. There are times when you need to make snap decisions. Even when that is the case, take three deep breaths and think with each breath before giving an answer.

7. Members of staff and community expect administrators to be solid and even-tempered. Appearing flustered or upset makes teachers more distrustful of your decisions. Deviations from that make an administrator suspect. Therefore, it is important to hear difficult things and not get rattled.

If there is some time when there is an emotional response to an issue, however, do not feel belittled. It is beneficial to staff and students alike to see administrators as human. It may help change the stereotype of administration for staff and community to see someone be emotionally appropriate and be a capable administrator. It is appropriate to laugh, cry, show anger, or be frustrated in different situations. Just do not let the emotions carry away the appropriate problem-solving thoughts.

8. Repeat only the positive parts of a story. It is the task of the administrator to create a positive atmosphere in a building. This is not to suggest becoming a Pollyanna. However, positive behavior begets other positive behavior. To turn the atmosphere of a building into a positive, healthy building, it is therefore necessary to concentrate on the positive. It is too easy to get caught up in the negative.

Do not talk about others negatively behind their back. Frame their actions in a manner that gives them credibility.

For example, a certain teacher intimidates students in the voice tone and using the words that he regularly uses. But he is actually insecure in his own skills and competence. When students complain about him, I am able to say that I know that is not what the teacher means because I have observed him in the classroom. I can discuss with students what happens in miscommunication between actual message and perceived message. I can frame it in a manner that leads to more understanding on the part of students and teacher. What is more important, I share this with the teacher so that he can be aware of how he is perceived.

9. When something happens, reframe it so that it becomes a positive. There is no such thing as a bad mistake, only one we do not learn from. If we do not learn the first time, we will recreate the mistake until we get the message. As administrators, it is our task to find out what message needs to be learned and then frame it in that perspective.

For example, a teacher came to me to discuss an overnight field trip. She had experienced several problems, some of which could have been serious. Luckily, none of them was. Instead of having her berate herself for what could have happened, we used the energy to come up with new procedures for next year to prevent any of these problems. We were able to figure out what lessons we learned from this event.

10. If there is a day or time when it is overwhelming, find an excuse to leave the building for a few minutes. Take something to the Central Office. Go visit a peer to discuss a committee. Find something to put things back into perspective. Tomorrow is always another day.

3

Maintaining Control of Your Time

As a teacher, the school day is dictated by bells and someone else's timetables. There is constant pressure to be on time, to finish the lesson before the bell rings, and to complete preparation during the prep hour. Because administrators do not have to adhere to the bell schedule as much as teachers, it is an assumption that an administrator has more flexibility in his or her personal schedule. There is even a secretary to keep a calendar, which leads to the assumption that the person has some control over the day.

That is true only to a degree. Most high school administrators spend from 60 to 80 hours a week performing their jobs. There are many constituents to consider, which means that many people have requests and demands on the time of this school leader. The day starts early and ends late because of evening commitments. There is work on weekends. One principal said it this way: "If you're a high school principal, you LIVE this job. You don't have a choice not to."

Teachers have a minimum day set by the contract. For administrators, however, the contract is not as clear. The term professionalism to describe job tasks can encompass a wide variety of duties, the same duties that create more demands on time as a person goes up the hierarchy within the system. Teachers have fewer demands than assistant principals. Assistants have fewer demands than head principals. There is no such thing as enough time.

Have You Got a Minute?

It is rare that a principal has a quiet minute to reflect. If a principal is in the office, there are people at the door or on the telephone. If a principal goes out into the halls, she or he is invariably greeted with the phrase, "Have you got a minute?" This phrase has to be the most deceptive phrase used by teachers. The minimizing of the time involved is a gentle way to get the attention of the administrator, knowing full well that few interactions, especially business interactions, take only a few minutes. That question implies an interaction that will take anywhere from 5 to 30 minutes. It does not take too many "Have you got a minute(s)?" to eat away the hours of the day.

The other phrase that is frequently used to get the attention of an administrator is "One quick question . . ." The question may be quick but the answer seldom is. If someone is asking an administrator a question, then there is some confusion to be cleared up or clarification to be given. That can rarely be done by a simple sentence. If it were that simple, the person would not have to be asking. Therefore, beware of simple questions because they beg for complicated, time-consuming answers.

One example is when the secretary asks what to do because there are not enough substitute teachers. Class coverage has to solved. Another problem is when food service needs to know how many students will be missing because of the field trips the next day. Maybe students come to find out how they can finance a student council retreat. There are few quick questions and even fewer quick answers.

Time is one of the most precious commodities for teachers and administrators alike. Because of the constant sense of passing time, teachers are always in a rush. They know they have to be somewhere soon. If they try to talk to an administrator in the 5 minutes between classes, they know they must be in the room ready to start when the bell rings. If they try to talk during lunch, they know that they will choke down their sandwich in 5 to 10 minutes, run off a test, and talk to the administrator within the 25-minute slot.

Most of the time pressures for an administrator come from interactions with people. Teachers have questions; students have concerns. Parents believe that schools are open to any drop-ins. They do not feel the need to make appointments as they would in a doctor's office. In addition, when they just drop in, it is usually with a problem and the parent is angry. They get doubly angry if they cannot be seen and take care of IMMEDIATELY. Because schools are public institutions, it is important to meet the needs of our populations. However, it is frustrating that there are so many demands.

It seems that interactions are largely on a demand basis. Teachers get frustrated with administrators if they do not have enough lead time. But the reciprocal does not seem to hold true. There are always a few teachers who are notorious for barely making deadlines, such as turning in grades on time or getting in their information for morning announcements. These are the same teachers who repeatedly open the door to the video studio with one important announcement when the students are already on the air delivering their messages. There is always a small group of teachers who will be late turning in their grades no matter how many days they have to do them. What would they do if students did that to them?

In the administrative offices, a closed door appears to mean nothing. When I was growing up, my mother taught me that a closed door indicated the need for privacy. If you needed the person on the other side of the door, you were required to knock and wait for a "Come in." Either most teachers did not have my mother or they have chosen to ignore their own mothers' admonitions. It is as though the closed door is meant for everyone but them because their issue is important and needs an answer. The daily urgency of teachers, the primacy of drop-in parent concerns, and the youth of students contributes to the fact that administrators often find their door opened without someone knocking or without their telling someone to come in.

Are people, particularly teachers, impolite or just rude? First, teachers are constantly under a time pressure, which creates a sense of urgency for their respective issues. They want to accomplish one task and get on to the next. Consequently, they interrupt conversations without even being aware of what they are doing. Second, because teaching is such an isolated task, teachers often feel that their issue is the most important. They do not have a sense of what other people are doing. Therefore, the primacy of their issue takes precedence over polite behavior. Third, schools function somewhat like a family in that the staff are a type of community. One tends to ignore the Emily Post rules of behavior in the less formal setting.

It seems as if there is no privacy in the administrative offices. Teachers will talk to a principal while he or she is having another conversation on the telephone. It is as though the administrator has two ears and can, therefore, listen to two things at once. Both ears, however, connect to only one brain! Interestingly, administrators become adept at doing several things at one time—listening on the telephone, listening to a person standing by their desk, and signing a pass all at once.

Day Planners

Most classes and workshops that discuss time management suggest buying a day planner and then writing every appointment and idea down. That linear, segmented method works for those people that I call "splitters." Such a person is good at maintaining an accurate date book and always carrying it with them. That person is good at seeing bits and pieces as opposed to the whole. Our society views that person as organized and efficient. Splitters are the type of administrators who schedule meetings and make them on time. They are formal about their appointments with staff. They will tell a teacher to make an appointment with the secretary or the administrator and may even carry their date book with them so they can schedule it immediately. They will be able to tell someone if a time is pre-scheduled with another appointment. Splitters keep important telephone numbers in alphabetical order in their rolodex. They may even have a card file to collect business cards of acquaintances.

There is another type of organizer that I call "a lumper." Such a person has piles that are grouped by importance. The most important piece of information is likely to be on top. There are piles on their desk and around the room by category. Registration information is in one pile, staff development is in another, and mail is in another.

If someone tries to organize the piles by putting some of the papers in manila folders by alphabetical order in a drawer, it would disorganize the "lumper." The lumper has difficulty keeping a day planner because appointments get scheduled and rescheduled. It is hard to keep the planner neat because those spaces are so tiny.

Pages that have the month at a glance are helpful to lumpers because she or he can see the entire month. But there is never enough room to write in those little squares so the information runs over between the days.

Lumpers will tell people to come in and talk without setting a definite time. They do not carry their date books with them. They try to remember in their head but that is a fallible method. Usually, they are good at juggling, but every once in a while they get trapped and must prioritize what is most important to do at that time. Lumpers may just throw all yellow telephone messages into one drawer throughout the year. They do not write the numbers in their book or on their rolodex because they know that if they need a telephone number, it is on one of those slips somewhere.

Neither style—splitting or lumping—is better than the other. Neither is more efficient although a blending of the two is probably best. No matter what, there will never be enough time in the day. If there were more than 24 hours in a day, there would just be more to do.

Just Say No

It is a necessary skill to learn to say no. Your presence will be wanted at all events and meetings. Attendance is indicative of support, which everyone wants from the building leader. It is not, however, possible to attend everything.

It is important, therefore, to set priorities. Attend each sport once throughout the season. Attend the music contests. Set priorities of which committees are to be a focus. Send the assistant principals to some meetings. Say no to others.

Schedule in the positive parts of being a principal. Go to the recognition ceremonies even though you may miss a meeting about asbestos removal. Others can handle that piece.

If you do not manage your time in a way that feels good to you, no one else will.

Suggestions for Handling Your Day

1. Interruptions are our business. Make a banner of this saying and hang it in the office. An administrator's job is to be of service to the school. People come for help, answers, consolation, to use you as a sounding board, and as a friend. On the other hand, because of

those interruptions, there are never two days that will be exactly the same. The job will never be boring. The interruptions and meetings all provide a richness and variety that most professions do not have.

2. Understand that a task will seldom be completed at one sitting. It may take two or three tries before it's done. Begin to see the demands and interruptions *as* the job, instead of distractions *to* the job. The reframing helps to realize that administrators are meant to serve others, as opposed to them serving you.

3. One of the best times to get things done, to clean off your desk, is an hour after school is over. Most urgent interactions have taken place during that first hour after school is out. During the next hour most people are out of the building and it is relatively quiet, even more so than before school. Most parents realize that school is over and do not try to call.

4. A way to make good use of time is to get a modem hook-up from home to school. There may be times when the most efficient use of time is to work an hour at home to accomplish an important task and access files at the school computer through the modem. An hour of uninterrupted work may replace a day of frustration at work.

5. On the other hand, it may be healthier to work hard at work and then go home and leave school in the school building. One of the fastest ways to wear down in administration is to be an administrator 7 days a week. Everyone, even God, needs a day of rest. Administrators need TWO. As much as possible, do not work on weekends. One principal I interviewed scheduled a massage every Friday at 3:00 p.m. Absolutely nothing interfered with that appointment.

6. Delegate!! It is not necessary to do everything yourself. It is not possible to do it all alone. That is why there is a staff of people to run a school. It is important to use people to develop their skills as well. Allow teachers to take on leadership roles.

7. Delegate, then let go. People who become administrators are often severe personal taskmasters. They expect things to be done well—maybe too well. It is crucial to realize that when tasks are delegated, things may be done differently. Some may not be done as well. Some tasks, however, may be done better. But if an administrator cannot let go, the task has not been truly delegated.

8. Decide what major issues you will tackle each year and stay focused on them. Let other new ideas wait until the focus idea is up

and running. If the building is doing strategic planning or future searching, concentrate on that for the year. If someone comes up with an idea for a new curriculum revision, suggest that that may have to wait until the strategic planning is done. There will always be new things to do, new ideas to promote. No one can do them all at one time, not even a principal.

9. Keep a list of ideas for future implementation that you may not have time for this year.

10. Let go. Let go. Let go. The job is important, and it is necessary to do a good job. One has to keep it in perspective, however—it is not the only thing that matters. In fact, one must constantly be reminded of what truly counts in this life.

11. Seek activities outside of education. It is crucial to stay balanced in the world apart from education to see how education fits and to get refreshed to do a good job while on the job.

12. Schedule a positive part of the job into each day and each week. If classroom observations are energizing, schedule them into your day. If walking the halls helps stay connected to students, write that on the schedule. If you leave the enjoyable tasks to "when I have the time," more pressing concerns will eat into that time.

13. Do not apologize for setting priorities. Many people will want attention. As the administrator, decide the focus of the building and your personal focus. Set priorities and explain to others that it is not possible to do everything.

14. Have fun!

4

Developing Your Emotional Teflon

"**N**o matter what you do, someone will not be happy." Take that quote, enlarge it, and hang it in the office. Do it in needlepoint or in charcoal or in oils. Because an administrator is always making decisions that affect many lives, it is impossible to have that kind of effect and make everyone happy—or sometimes make them even mildly content. In fact, if everyone is happy, then the principal is probably not doing the job.

Those who are most unhappy are most likely to scream first and loudest. An issue that is very important to teachers is the types of classes and hours they will teach throughout a day. The master schedule is the foundation of the school. Taking away a last hour prep from a teacher who has had that prep hour for several years will mean that teacher will be in the office complaining as soon as the schedule is public.

The opposite, however, is seldom true. People seldom run to the office to tell someone how happy they are or to say thank you for the prep hour they requested. Certainly, there are those who go out of their way to be positive, to say thank you, and to talk about good things, but it seems to be true in a school that the bad news comes first and loudest. In a school, no news is truly good news.

Emotional Teflon

Because so much of what an administrator hears is negative, it is difficult to stay upbeat. One needs to develop what I call *emotional teflon*. As an administrator, one needs to be aware of feelings and issues, but one must develop the ability to let negativity slide off. It is important to be aware of personal feelings, but it is important to keep them from ruling. There are times when it is necessary to put a Plexiglas window between the head and the heart. Although it is necessary to see what each is doing, it is important not to let either one be the supreme decision maker.

As an administrator, people come with problems, both personal and professional. People come because they are unhappy or discontent and need something fixed or solved. Therefore, much of your day will be spent with negativity. For example, a teacher comes before school complaining that no one rousts the morning smokers from the front of the building. Another teacher complains that the speakers are not working in his homeroom so he cannot hear announcements. Another complains that there are too many students in the hall when they should be in homeroom. This all takes place with the first "Good morning" of the day. Next, a parent descends on the office before school complaining that her child has missed a class ten times and she was never notified. The parent is angry at the teacher, the school, and, finally, the student, in the reverse order that it should be. Few other occupations begin the day with such a negative jump-start.

It is hard not to let it get to you because there will always be something wrong for someone in your building. There will be certain members of the staff who will always have a negative comment to say, no matter what. It is hard to realize that there is nothing that will satisfy those persons, no matter how hard you try. Unfortunately, it is usually these teachers who are the most vocal at staff meetings. Those teachers who are in agreement with administration and the policies often just quietly tend to business.

For example, a teacher complains if memos are not sent out in timely fashion and points up any typing errors. This same teacher is the one who complains in staff meetings about lack of administrative follow-through. It can become a standard joke in the office that if there have been no complaints from that teacher, then the memo must be satisfactory.

These nay-saying people will have something to say about every policy, every meeting, and every event. Many times, the policies have absolutely nothing to do with them. In situations such as those, it is difficult to remember that every behavior has a purpose. The person may not realize what he or she is doing. Chronic complainers, such as the one mentioned above, are not happy people. Their self-definition may come from deciding what they are *not*, as opposed to what they *are*. Therefore, they need to set up all kinds of situations in which they are the fault-finders or have the contrary opinion. It is their goal to be opposite, in order to have a role. Unfortunately, such behavior becomes wearing and draining. It is human to want to avoid that person. It is possible to avoid walking in their part of the hall just to avoid any complaints.

It is sad to realize that such negativity develops an impetus. It tends to feed on itself. It may be necessary to deal with such a person on a one-to-one basis to find out what is really going on. Is she or he unhappy personally? Does she or he have a grudge against the administration? Is this person a perpetual malcontent?

In a building with a large staff, there will naturally be more such people than with a small staff. It seems that negativity grows geometrically with the size of the staff.

The complaints will come. Be forewarned. At every staff meeting, there will be someone who will bring up a surprise issue. When that happens, the response has two parts. One, is there some validity in the expressed concern? If so, then deal with it. Two, if the real issue is not the expressed one and is merely the constant negativity of the person, then use a delaying tactic. Let the person know that the complaint is heard, then move on to the next topic. It is allowable not to act on every single concern expressed by a staff.

Sometimes, however, such complaints "hook" the administrator because there is a kernel of truth in the complaint, but the complainant is being negative only for the sake of being negative. For example, the high school is under construction. Some people are having trouble with allergies and air quality. A certain teacher is complaining constantly at staff meetings about going to OSHA or making it a union issue. This person, not a union rep or department chair, does not have allergies but merely enjoys stirring things up. An administrator has to develop the teflon and let his or her negativity slide off even though the issue of air quality must be dealt with. It is sometimes difficult to separate the issue from the persistently negative person. A human tendency is to say, "That is just so-and-so," when there may truly be an issue to deal with.

Administrative Burnout

Some administrators who are described as "burnt out" are often those who are accused of not listening to what teachers, students, and parents have to say. They are the ones who seem not to care. It is as though they are completely disconnected from feelings, particularly the feelings of understanding and empathy. They have heard the same complaints so frequently and over such a period of time that they have become distanced as a self-protection.

Anytime a person is at the top of the hierarchy of an organization, he or she will be subjected to many of the same comments and complaints repeated over and over because of the number of people below him or her who have never experienced certain facets of the organization. For example, parents of incoming ninth graders who come to registration are experiencing a new facet in their own personal growth because they may never have parented high school students before. The concerns, fears, procedures, and joys are new for them. For someone who has taught and then been an administrator, however, the cycle keeps repeating. The questions are the same. "How does homeroom work?" The comments are the same. "This building is so big. How will my student know where to go?" It is easy to lose sight of the fact that this is a new experience for some even though it may be an oft-repeated occurrence for others.

Because patterns repeat, an administrator may appear to be laissez-faire about a concern that alarms a parent or student. People may accuse the administrator of not taking them seriously. Parents may misread an administrator's emotional distance to mean that the administrator does not care. The distance represents the ability of the administrator to develop teflon that lets feelings come close without sticking.

Instead of using the repeated patterns to make a person disconnected, that awareness can be used to pre-empt problems or forewarn people. It is the total experience of an administrator that can be used as an asset to suggest remedies that have worked for other people. The key is to remember that an administrator has a more global picture. It is important to respect the emotions of other people and yet maintain the ability to use experience and wisdom to do what is right.

There are times when it is appropriate to let concerns slide off. For example, for the twentieth time, the science department complains that the administrators do not follow through on discipline. The first task is to find out if it is true. If so, then administrators need to be held accountable. If not, the administrator must communicate to the science department what has actually been happening and recognize that for some people, that will never be enough. There is never enough discipline or communication.

Developing the Teflon— Dilemma or Problem

How does one develop emotional teflon? One of the first steps is to deciding if the issue at hand is a dilemma or a problem. Larry Cuban (1996) of Stanford University delineates between the two. *Dilemmas* are issues for which there is no solution. They can only be managed. Attendance is a dilemma. No matter how many parent newsletters go home, or phone calls are made, or detentions are assigned, or attendance policies are formulated, there will never be perfect attendance. Attendance in school by students—and teachers, for that matter—is determined by many factors, most of which the school cannot control. If a family does not have a value that says school attendance is important, there is little the school can do. Certainly, the student can be placed in detention, there can be parent conferences stressing the importance of school, and the student can receive poor grades as an outcome. But if the student and parent do not have the internal value that supports school attendance, school policies cannot have a lasting effect.

School policies become a management tool to assist teachers in dealing with the student's academic progress. A student must be in class to learn. If a student misses a lot and is not, for example, in class for more than half a marking period, it makes sense that the student has not gotten the information and cannot pass. In the world of work, a person cannot show up for work 50% of the time and expect to earn a full salary.

An administrator must deal honestly with both parent and student to let them know what the school can and cannot do. Many parents get angry because their child's school attendance has been a dilemma for them as well. They hope it could be a problem for the school that the school could thereby solve. However, it does not work that way.

This dilemma and others like it can only be managed. Attendance can be shaped and structured by policies, late passes, detention, or failure, but it will never be solved by such policies. To believe that an administrator can fix this issue is to set the administrator up for emotional turmoil.

A *problem* can be identified as a situation for which solutions exist. An example of a problem is when the guidance counselor needs more rooms for administering schoolwide testing standardized achievement tests. Each teacher needs a quiet room. Even if some teachers have to meet in the cafeteria or a nearby church, there is a solution. It may not make everyone happy, but that is not the criteria for a solution.

How to frame a problem depends on the perspective. What is solvable to some people may not be solvable to others. A teacher has difficulty getting her students to class on time. She complained to the principal that students are always tardy. She sends the students to their administrator for detention. She calls the parents. She does not see a solution. Her prime concern is the constant disruption for her other students.

For the administrator, this is a problem that can be solved by the teacher locking her door when the bell rings. Then if a student is in the hall and should not be there, the security monitor will send them to in-school suspension.

However, another problem arises because the student misses class and must be responsible for the missing work. That becomes a problem for the teacher. The teacher defined the issue as a problem because the late student was causing a disruption. The administrator gave one solution. That solution, however, caused another problem even if the initial one was solved.

If, however, the teacher defined the tardiness as a dilemma because the tardiness was disruptive to the class's learning and to the student, then a different strategy might have to be devised. Problems beg for solutions, dilemmas must be managed. If one problem erupts after the solution, perhaps the issue should be reframed as a dilemma.

Part of the process of deciding between dilemma and problem is listening to what people have to say and hearing the real message. Students who smoke in front of the building before school may be considered a problem if the issue is upholding rules to make a visible show of concern for the climate of the school. If that is the issue, then an administrator can pay attention to the smokers themselves. If the issue is that the same teacher complains about the smokers in front because she or he does not feel that the monitors are doing their job appropriately, then the issue becomes the smokers and the monitors. Are the monitors supposed to be out in front in the morning? It may be necessary to meet with them and brainstorm more effective ways of patrolling the school. However, it may be that the complainant is one of the constant nay-sayers who wants to voice his or her perpetual discontent. If that is the case, then listen to what is true and let go of the rest. There may be many more pressing concerns than smokers.

Certainly, having smokers in front of the building is not desirable. One technique is to stand there occasionally and confront the smokers personally. It may be appropriate to do what Neal Nickerson, University of Minnesota professor, says to do, which is to "use deceit and sly cunning." The sly cunning is to decide what is important. Although it may feel good to tell the teacher to just quit complaining, instead, one acknowledges the complaint and quietly goes on to more important business.

Too often, we treat human issues as though they are problems, when, in fact, they are dilemmas. The faulty definition leads to needless emotional stress. If an issue has solutions, it is a problem. When the secretary says there are not enough substitute teachers, that is a problem. Someone has to be found to cover each class.

If, however, this becomes an ongoing issue, then it is a dilemma that begs other interventions. Are there not enough people available? Is it that teachers do not call for a replacement in time? Are people gone too often? If there are many answers and none of them is clearcut, it's a dilemma. Dilemmas often require the interaction of many factors, none of which will solve the issue by itself. To revisit an earlier situation, instituting an attendance policy will help provide a framework, but it will not solve the fact that some students do not make it to school.

The hard part is to let go. We have the mistaken belief that we, as teachers and as administrators, are trained people who can fix things and solve problems. Sometimes, that is not true. There are many daily events over which we have no control. We can only do our best, define the issue, initiate and follow through with our plan, and then let go.

Active Listening

Listening with your head and heart combined is part of developing a way to stay involved with, and yet detached from, the issues of a building. Are the words expressed the real concern? Or is there some underlying issue? What is the real purpose of the behavior? Is the negativity purposeful? Does it have a point that can be used to improve the school? Is there anything that can be done? Sometimes, no. For example, if teachers are complaining about the superintendent, the only thing to do is listen. Ultimately, it is not the function of the principal to change the superintendent. The only person one can truly change is oneself. Even that is difficult.

Many times, people just want to vent. They may know that nothing can be done, but they want to tell someone who has power. These conversations often start out with' "Just so you know. . . . " Often, there is nothing to be done except listen and store the information on the "great computer disk of life."

An administrator needs to decide what the real issue is, frame it as problem or dilemma, and then decide if it merits intervention. Is there anything that should be done? Is there time to do it, who should do it, and when? Make those decisions, delegate, and then let it go. Let the teflon work.

Suggestions for Developing Teflon

1. Know yourself. Establish goals personally and professionally that are in line with personal standards and values. Then listen to what people have to say and decide if what they are complaining about has merit. Decide to do something about the whole issue, part of it, or none. Then congratulate yourself for the decision.

2. Pretend you have a piece of Plexiglas between head and heart. When dealing with constant complaints, sit down, and think about the issues with the imaginary Plexiglas in place. See the feelings

associated with the heart are in place; it is not necessary to "feel" them to know they are there. Then deal with the issue with the head knowing that the emotional part of the heart can be accessed, if necessary.

3. Understand that there is no such thing as a bad mistake, only one not learned from. When something happens, think "What gift did I get from this experience?" By reframing it as something positive, it will become a learning experience instead of a put-down.

4. Stay fresh so that no matter how many times the same complaint comes up, there will still be an understanding that this is a concern for the presenter, who does not realize that this same story has been expressed by many other people. It is difficult to remember that others do not have the same global perspective as an administrator.

5. Practice listening for the real issue that is under what people are saying. That often takes time. When people start talking about an issue, they begin with the part that is closest to the surface and makes them the least vulnerable. It will take time to get to the part of the issue that is the true source of the conflict. (There is more on this listening in Chapter 5.)

6. Practice defining issues as problems or dilemmas. Remember that problems beg solutions, dilemmas can only be managed.

7. Exercise. Read. Play music. Walk. Do whatever it takes to keep the teflon from getting scratched.

Maybe You Should Wear a Striped Shirt

Refereeing Conflict

Referees in many athletic contests wear black-and-white striped shirts so they are readily identified as they declare "foul," "out," or "safe." Maybe an administrative uniform should include wearing a striped shirt because so much of what an administrator does is to mediate and referee conflict.

Of the hundreds of interactions throughout the day, most of them deal with some type of conflict.

- Pao wants more money from the Gifted/Talented budget, but the coordinator does not believe that he needs it. A principal gets to mediate and explain to the Gifted/Talented Coordinator why Pao needs that money.

- Marie and Avante, two guidance counselors, have an argument over who is responsible for the guidance office newsletter. The department chair calls the principal in as mediator to resolve the differences because the tiff is having an effect on the whole department.

- DaShawn had a verbal altercation with a teacher about a grade. The principal mediates between teacher and student.

- Ms. Hopkins is in the office demanding a 504 plan (a federally funded program similar to an Individual Education Plan) for her daughter, who has Attention Deficit Hyperactivity Disorder (ADHD). But the child has not been officially diagnosed by a physician and cannot have service until that is done. Ms. Hopkins has consulted a private advocate group, which has told her to be forceful and demand that an assessment take place. The advocates did not make it clear to Ms. Hopkins, however, that the child needs a medical assessment before the school can implement any label, such as ADHD. The principal gets to negotiate between the interests of the four parties—student, parent, school, and advocate group.

- The secretary is upset because Mr. Alvarez refused to answer his telephone in the early morning to avoid being asked to cover a class when there were not enough substitutes that day. The secretary wants the principal to talk to Mr. Alvarez.

- At the staff meeting, the administrator has the task of sharing news from Central Office at the staff meeting that the district has decided that there will be mandatory sexual harassment training for all district employees. Each employee must take part in a seminar for one full day before the school year ends. There are three training session opportunities for which staff must sign up. Staff members feel that they know enough about harassment. They do not want to be out of their class for an entire day for something they see as a waste of time. The teachers are frustrated, and the principal must listen to their complaints. Ultimately, there is nothing to do but listen. A good administrator can see both sides of the issue but must support the district mandates. That, however, creates fallout in the building that must also be dealt with.

The list goes on and on.

Conflict is a part of normal daily life. But teachers go into the profession because they want to teach. They like students and are excited about their content areas. They want to be liked and respected by students and coworkers alike. They do not, however, want to deal with conflict. They perceive that discipline and angry parents are the domain of assistant principals and principals.

Teachers want conflict to be resolved in the office, far away from their classroom. In fact, most teachers fear an angry parent more than anything else because they were never trained in how to deal with anger or conflict. There is no university program that I know of that trains teachers and/or administrators in ways to resolve disputes or how to defuse anger. Yet so much of daily life with other human beings will inherently involve conflictual situations.

Administrators enter their jobs with the notion that they will be responsible for curricular issues, teacher evaluations, supervision of school activities, dealing with parents, and dealing with discipline and attendance issues. But I am not aware of any training program that prepares administrators for the amount and types of conflict that will besiege them.

Issues that are brought to an administrator are encrusted with feelings and vested interests. Heartfelt issues become even more difficult to deal with because the combatants cannot divorce themselves from their opinion long enough to see from the other person's perspective. The issues that are not as value-laden and emotional are often not even brought to the office. Therefore, the issues that come to administrators are often difficult.

The hierarchy of schools is inverted when it comes to dealing with conflict. Administrators are at the bottom. Teachers have some conflict to manage, but the degree and amount of conflict increases in a geometric proportion at the administrative level. By the time a principal gets home, she or he does not even want to hear the cats yowling at each other.

Such continual conflict takes its toll.

As an administrator, it is difficult because not every issue can be resolved. Issues cannot always be resolved to the satisfaction of all constituents. No one said administration would be neat and orderly. No one said that a good administrator should have a neat desk and a Garrison Keillor Lake Woebegone school.

It is symptomatic of a conflictual situation for a disputant to blame and project responsibility on to someone or something else. When a person makes a pointing gesture, it is important to pay attention to the three fingers pointing back at the owner. Pointing outward helps absolve someone from his or her own part in dealing with the situation. But it also cheats the person of the opportunity to reflect and change his or her own behavior.

There are those who are "conflict junkies," similar to the "anger junkies" described in Chapter 1. They seem to create conflict, personally and professionally, no matter where they go. They get hooked on the endorphin high that comes from the rush of adrenaline that is produced during fights, fits of temper, and angry outbursts. They do not want to take the time to resolve issues because it takes a lot of work. They are the ones who are in the office complaining about issues that have nothing to do with them or their department. They complain about every memo. They always have a negative comment at every staff meeting. There is nothing that pleases them.

It may be necessary to establish some kind, but firm, boundaries so that these people do not eat up a lot of time.

It is particularly difficult to deal with perpetual strife when one is tired and worn out. When things are going well, it is easier to anticipate some of the negativity and conflict before it happens.

There are many challenges involved in dealing with conflict. It takes a skilled, empathic listener to deal with conflict and facilitate mediation. There is satisfaction in reframing conflicts so that there can be resolution. There is excitement in being able to solve problems. There is also creativity in finding ways to manage dilemmas.

Levels of Conflict

There are different levels of conflict.

Level One Conflict

Level One contains those issues that can be dealt with relatively quickly. For example, the enrollment clerk has difficulty with Ms. Vujovich because she refuses to turn in her grade sheets on time. If she does not, the entire process of scanning and printing grades is held up. This conflict is easy to resolve because there is an obvious bottom line. Therefore, an administrator can let Ms. Vujovich know that she must turn them in and explain why it is important. If she continues to be delinquent, it is an issue of insubordination and can be dealt with by district policy.

For Level One conflict, there is a right and wrong. Issues can be resolved by appealing to policy, laws, or commonly held values. For example, it is wrong for someone to hit another person. It is illegal to go through a red light. It is right that someone returns a stolen textbook. People, especially those who break society's rules, may disagree, but there is consensus about the ethos of the culture and building.

Level Two Conflict

Level Two conflict is more involved. There is a difference of opinion or values that is not clearcut and there is some credibility on the part of each combatant. The perennial "he said, she said" type of arguments would fit this category.

For example, two students have a fight over what one said about the other. There may be hurt feelings involved. The issue could have started months ago over a broken friendship. It could be that one of them is going out with the other's former boyfriend/girlfriend. They may have called each other names. The conflict is not clearcut, and the resolution involves admission of error by both parties.

This conflict takes time to resolve. The following conflict resolution strategies are helpful.

1. First, there must be a mediator—often an administrator in the school—who will listen to both sides. The mediator may listen to each side separately or jointly, so that each of the combatants can hear the other person's side.

2. Then the mediator needs to paraphrase to make certain that the real issue is out in the open. If each person agrees that the paraphrasing sums up the concern, the mediator can proceed. If not, then the mediator needs to ask further questions until clarity and honesty are reached.

3. When the issue is on the table, the mediator may need to probe even further to get at any underlying issues. What comes out first in a conflictual situation is usually just a surface issue. For Level two conflicts, the problem has built up over time, and it will take time to probe for any underlying roots.

4. When the entire issue is out in the open, it is time to ask each person what it would take for the conflict to be over. Both parties need to state what they need. Then each party has to be able to fulfill that expectation. If they can, the conflict can be resolved. If not, the mediator will need to back up and reframe until each person is satisfied. If the issue is not correctly defined, one or more of the parties will not be able to give up the struggle.

5. A final closure activity is to get each person to agree that the conflict is over and done with. For students, it is helpful at this point to give them pointers on what to say to their friends if the friends try

to stir it up again. It may be helpful to let them know what would happen if the conflict does crop up again so that the expectations are clear.

It often takes 45 to 60 minutes to mediate such occurrences and do it well. It takes 10 to 15 minutes to get the surface issues on the table. It may take another 5 to 10 minutes to get at the real issue lying below the surface. Then each person needs a few minutes to state what he or she needs. Each person needs a few minutes to think and, agree or disagree. It takes a few minutes to restate what each person has agreed to before he or she leaves the session. That is a total of about an hour. When school is in session for only 6 to 7 hours a day, it is easy to see how one conflict can eat away the time. It is not unusual to deal with several such conflicts during a week.

Level Two conflicts took time to develop and they take time to resolve because the conflict is over issues that are value-laden and, therefore, emotional. The process of coming to a solution that both people can live with cannot be rushed. If someone treats a Level two conflict as though it were Level one, the conflict will resurface. For example, if two students are fighting and come to the office, simply telling them that fighting is not allowed, suspending them, and sending them home will merely put the conflict on hold. Just telling someone to stop it—contrary to the belief of Nancy Reagan's Just Say No campaign—rarely works, particularly with students. There is a strong likelihood that the conflict will resurface either in the community or in school. It may even get worse, particularly if students drag their friends into it.

For adults, such conflicts may go underground. If two teachers do not get along, instead of openly fighting as students may do, they tend to be more passive-aggressive. There may be innuendoes in the lounge. There may be snide comments. It may lead to open hostility.

Such conflict is detrimental to the morale of a staff. If an administrator knows about a long-standing conflict, it is better to bring the parties in to discuss it. Some administrators ignore such conflict, assuming that the teachers are adults and can deal with their own problems. Unfortunately, most adults are not good at dealing with conflict. They tend to avoid it and merely push it underground, which causes the disharmony to fester and come out in other ways.

Disagreements are a healthy part of a human institution. Healthy relationships must have a chance to experience and resolve conflict. Unhealthy conflict acts like a fungus and grows in dark places. It is the task of an administrator to facilitate the resolution of the fungal conflicts.

For example, one department had a group of people who constantly sniped at each other at meetings. The comments were about personalities, as opposed to differences of philosophies. Conflicts were never aired publicly but only to small groups of people behind closed doors. Everyone knew that certain members of the department did not like each other, but no one wanted to work it out. They were afraid of hurting someone's feelings and making other people angry. Therefore, no one communicated, they avoided each other, and eventually, some left the school.

A certain amount of turmoil can be the impetus to a new understanding and a healing. When people are comfortable, however, they do not change. Therefore, a difference of opinion can lead to growth and change if people are willing to deal with the conflict directly. It is then that conflict may precipitate a healthy change.

It is important to use the resources on the staff to deal with such issues. Social workers, counselors, assistant principals, and chemical dependency counselors are all invaluable persons to use. There is no way that an administrator can resolve all the issues that arise in a school. Because schools are people business and people create turmoil, there will always be a need for skilled conflict managers.

Level Three

Level Three conflict may not be able to be solved. It may be a dilemma as opposed to a problem, as discussed in the previous chapter. Because dilemmas are rich in complexity, there may not be a permanent solution.

An example of a Level Three conflict is when the district office allows too many students to enroll in the building. There are other high schools in the district that have space. The school is known for the quality of its programs, many parents have requested it, and the district wants to make parents happy. Unfortunately, the building is cramped. Teachers are complaining about the class size. The halls are crowded. Everyone from food service to assistant principals is feeling overwhelmed.

The district wants to allow parents to have their choice of schools to satisfy the wishes of the community. The staff of the school, however, wants to deliver a high-quality program without being overwhelmed. Their perception is that a crowded school is not educationally sound. Both groups have their reasons for their stances.

This conflict is a dilemma that can only be managed, not solved. An administrator must make adjustments to accommodate the crowding. It may be necessary to add an extra lunch period. Some teachers will have to be itinerant, that is, not have their own classroom. Other teachers will have to share their rooms with the roving teachers. Teachers will have to order more books.

Because there is no simple resolution and the effect of such a situation is pervasive, there will be repercussions throughout the school year. There will be more discipline referrals. It will be impossible to get all the ninth graders in the auditorium at one time so any ninth-grade assembly will have to be held in two sessions.

Level Three conflict is a dilemma that must be managed by a variety of methods. It is frustrating, however, because the conflict appears in so many different arenas. Lower-level conflicts are easier to deal with. However, much of what happens in school is a Level Two or three conflict. Both take time, are exhausting, and are stress-producing.

Hawthorne Effect

Some dilemmas may improve simply because of the attention paid to them, otherwise known as the Hawthorne Effect. If people believe that their efforts are valuable, then things change merely from the attention paid to the issue. There are signs posted on Minneapolis city streets that say "Accident-Free Zone." Studies showed that there were fewer accidents in those areas. People wondered if there were more police patrols, lower speed limits, or more stoplights. Nothing had changed except for the signs; yet the accident rate decreased in those high accident-prone areas. The Hawthorne Effect was in effect.

Sometimes, school issues work themselves out because someone paid attention. Attendance is a good example. There is no easy answer to the problem of getting students to school on time. Teachers will feel validated, however, if an attendance committee is formed, policies are changed, or new ideas developed because it acknowledges their daily struggle in getting students to class so they can learn. Some of the changes may promote better attendance, some may not.

The staff perceives that the administrators will devote energy to that which the administrator sees as important. If an administrator wants to resolve a conflict between members of a department, it will be perceived that resolution of conflict is an important issue. If an administrator ignores such a conflict, it will be perceived that the administrator does not put that as a high priority.

In the eyes of the staff, it is important to choose issues wisely. Merely paying attention to an issue may help the problem get resolved.

Conflict is normal. When people are comfortable, they become complacent and have no impetus to do anything any differently. It is only when someone becomes uncomfortable that there is motivation to change. Therefore, conflict can be seen as a powerful change agent. Instead of fighting it, we can embrace it as a means to a new beginning.

Suggestions for Surviving the Conflict

1. Learn how to resolve conflict, if that is unfamiliar. Read books such as *Getting Past No: Negotiating with Difficult People* by William Ury (1991) or *Getting to Yes* by Roger Fisher and William Ury (1991).

2. Learn to define issues as dilemmas or problems. The method of framing the issue will determine the initiatives toward its solution.

3. When dealing with angry or upset people, realize that the first important step is to listen. What they really want is someone to hear their viewpoint.

4. Conflict is a healthy part of life. There is no avoiding it. Conflict is like the earthquakes that take place along the San Andreas Fault. There is conflict in the movement of the tectonic plates. When the plates move, something has to be resolved. The earth shakes, realigns itself, and some things fall apart. Yet the quake causes people to rebuild, work together, and come to new understanding.

5. In dealing with conflict "junkies," schedule them at a time when there is a limited amount of time to listen. Put firm boundaries on them and yet acknowledge their concerns. It could be damaging in the teacher network if they perceive they are being brushed off, but it is not necessary to give them all the time they seem to believe they need.

6. Recognize that conflict gives us lessons to learn. The conflict is a process that moves us along to a mature understanding of, and ability to work with, people.

Everything You Didn't Know About Adult Learners

6

A relatively recent cultural awareness examines the importance of adult learning stages. Lifelong learning has become important as the so-called baby boomer generation advances through the stages of life. There is a larger population of adult learners than ever before. Adults are conducting mature lives to live longer with more options and more resources than ever before. Stages of adulthood are being examined in a way we have never examined them.

The idea of stages of adult psychosocial development was popularized by writers such as Gail Sheehy, author of *Passages* in 1976 and by Dan Levinson, author of *The Seasons of a Man's Life* (1978). Sheehy observed that men and women experienced the same stages of adult development, albeit asynchronously. She believed that there appeared to be more "outer restrictions and inner contradictions for women during the first half of life" (p. 19). The opposite appeared to be true for men. This was important because Sheehy believed that the "prizes of our society" tend to be for outer, not inner achievement. It is important to look at the differences between men and women, particularly as nontraditionals, such as women, enter administration.

Levinson's work, done with 40 adult men, described four stages of development. The stages were

Stage One—childhood and adolescence from ages 3 to 17;

Stage Two—early adulthood from ages 22 to 40;

Stage Three—middle adulthood from age 45 to 60;

Stage Four—late adulthood beyond the age of 65.

Between each stage, he described a phenomenon he called "transition" that functioned as a time to reflect on the previous stage and to prepare for the next one. The transitions, a particularly important time, lasted from 4 to 5 years.

It is important to understand the stages of adult development because teachers and staffs within our buildings may be experiencing any of the stages from two through four. In Stage Two, adults are in the "greatest contradiction and stress" (p. 22). Adults are struggling to find their place societally and personally. This is the time of coupling, raising families, investing in homes, and getting further education. It is a time of great accomplishments and great frustrations.

Stage Three, middle adulthood, brings a change. This is the time that some people have called a "mid-life crisis" when they begin to realize that there is a shift in life. Human bodies begin to wear down. Professionally, many people have reached a peak of satisfaction in what they do. Families may be growing up and leaving home. It is the time when people begin to look toward retirement and the calming of life, instead of looking toward challenges and excitement.

Stage Four brings people to retirement, to leaving a profession that has defined their identity, and to facing physical ailments. It is exciting to some and dreadful to others. Before the baby boomer generation, people saw retirement as a time when people sat in their rocker or played in their garden until death released them from life.

However, this generation of mature adults continues to learn, to be involved in careers that they could not pursued when they had to support a family. Studies have shown that people who stay physically fit and mentally active can lead active, productive lives well into their 80s and 90s.

As administrators, we will deal with learners at all stages of development, from our students in Stage one to the adults in the other three stages. In our training, we learned about students in Stage one. We learned nothing about the other three stages in which most of our current constituents are!!!

Not only are we uneducated about adult stages of emotional development, but we have little awareness of the adult learner. In the 1970s, Malcolm Knowles used the work of Piaget and Erikson to study the adult learner (Knowles, 1990). He recognized that adults learn best with what he called "self-directed inquiry." His self-directed inquiry is the constructivism of the 1990s, meaning that learners will construct meaning though personal inquiry.

Adult learners are autonomous and self-directed. They want to learn what they see as useful, either personally or professionally. As an administrator, one needs to promote such exploration by knowing what the staff wants to learn. It then is incumbent to provide opportunities that pique their interest. Meshing the needs of the district, building, and individuals will require getting to know the staff as individuals and as departments.

Adult learners have a foundation of life experiences from which to draw. The best adult learning occurs when that foundation is acknowledged and then expanded. Too often, schools look outside of the district to bring in "experts" for training when there is frequently a person on the staff or in the district who may have the necessary expertise. Using this resource is empowering to the individual and the staff because it recognizes the adult for what he or she has accomplished.

Adults want to know what they are going to get out of any situation. What is the goal? How is any new program going to impact their daily life? Is it going to mean more work? More paperwork? Therefore, it is crucial to give teachers the global perspective before beginning any training session.

Teachers are utilitarian and practical in that they want relevant information that will enhance their ability to teach. They do not want to be bothered by "fluff." They prefer training sessions that help them take something back to the classroom for immediate implementation. They will say that the most valuable trainings are those in which they get a concrete handout or idea that can be used immediately. In college courses, they will take ideas wholesale and use them. They will take handouts, copy them, and distribute them in their classrooms. They do not want to have to rework or adapt something. That is not necessarily the best example of learning, however.

Adults do not want to waste time. Time is seen as a teacher's most valuable commodity because a teacher never has enough time to get all the curriculum covered or papers graded. Therefore, any training session should begin promptly and end early. If given the choice, teachers will often opt for a shorter lunch break so they can get out early. It is important to treat adult learners with respect, which can be done by using time wisely, providing information meaningful for adults, acknowledging their expertise, and honoring their time pressure.

Adult learners must be kept busy and must be honored for different learning styles, just like the students. For example, at a staff meeting it is important to present items succinctly, both orally and visually. It is important to model consideration for different learning styles that should be replicated by teachers in the classroom. There should be visual, auditory, and kinesthetic opportunities to practice what teachers need to know. There should be large group work and small group work. There should be opportunities to move around.

Teachers have less tolerance for boredom than do students. If doing staff development, remember that the learning curve in time is particularly crucial for adult learners. The first 20 minutes of a 50-minute lesson are the most important, followed by the last 10 minutes for review. The middle 20 minutes are the low point of learning. Structure an activity at that low point so that the adults are practicing what they are learning with a hands-on project. They could be brainstorming in a small group, listing ideas, or compiling data. The important part is to keep them engaged and active.

Adults need a physical break every hour so that they get up and move around, because teachers are not used to sitting still. They are less patient than their students. Do not expect them to sit any longer than 45 to 50 minutes without a break.

It is difficult to get adults to refocus after a break. It is particularly difficult to keep them awake right after lunch if they are just sitting. Never show a video right after the lunch break or some of the teachers will fall asleep. Use this time for group work, visuals, brainstorming, and movement, just as a good teacher would with students in a classroom. Brainstorming may be enhanced by using big sheets of paper and colored markers—particularly the smelly ones. As an administrator, it is necessary to model the behavior of active, engaged learning. With the awareness of Howard Gardner's Multiple Intelligence Theory, we need to implement strategies for learners, whether they are 6 years old or 60, to learn and demonstrate their knowledge in a variety of ways.

It is not uncommon for teachers to be doing two things at one time, particularly at staff meetings, because of their sense of time pressures. Therefore, if they feel they can do two things at one time, such as correct papers and listen at a staff meeting, they will. Although some people find that rude, it may not be insulting. However, it will be a constant struggle to run staff meetings as involved, instructional opportunities in which teachers feel so engaged they do not even want to grade papers. Sometimes, adult learners need to be challenged to learn things they think they do not need to know. Because so much of their personal learning experiences have been passive, most adults are intimidated by active learning in the form of role plays, artistic displays, or group work. Adults have not all been trained in effective cooperative learning. It may be necessary to provide such opportunities for staff and then process the experience afterward.

Talking about how people learn, metacognition, is an important part of teaching, whether working with adults or children. It is important to provide opportunities to hear from other people and reflect on best practices. Structuring time for metacognition with teachers is what we would wish teachers to do for students in a classroom. When people know how they learn best, they are more likely to use that habit consciously to learn more.

Suggestions for Working With Adult Learners:

1. Send out agendas prior to meetings and stick to them. Start and end the meetings on time—ending early is even better.

2. Be well prepared for any meeting. Have background materials ready if necessary.

3. Be excited about what you are presenting. It is important that you believe in what you are doing. If you do not, neither will your teachers.

4. Provide a wide variety of learning opportunities for your teachers. Suggest conferences. Photocopy articles from journals that may pique their interest or support what they do.

5. Be supportive with time and money as much as possible. Giving teachers the gift of time is one of the most valuable resources to give them. If there is a district workshop day, schedule half of the day for a training, and schedule in some time when teachers can meet with their departments to share ideas. Give them time to collaborate,

to share, to develop their ideas. Then get out of their way and let them do what they do best—TEACH.

6. Treat the teachers as human beings. Get to know something about each one. Who has children? Who travels? Who reads? Teachers are like students—they will work very hard and will even do things they do not want to do if they respect their teacher/leader. Find out what talents each may be able to share or demonstrate to the other staff members. If someone is well-trained in authentic assessment, have him or her facilitate a workshop.

7. Consciously structure opportunities for the staff to stretch by using visuals, role plays, or other active forms of learning. Adults are more afraid of doing such activities than students because their experience with learning has been much more passive. It is up to the administrator to take people out of their comfort zone.

8. If meetings are long, provide frequent breaks. One 5-minute break per hour is helpful. Provide some nourishing treats as refreshments. Teachers particularly like fruit or juice in the afternoon. So often, treats are provided in the morning of a session but not in the afternoon. A little snack brings up the blood sugar and sets a caring atmosphere.

7

Looking Into the Mirror of Humor

Humor is emotional chaos remembered in tranquility.

James Thurber

Who said "Most of life is just showing up?" Comedians make people laugh by taking daily events and accenting the unusual parts. Think of the material for Rosie O'Donnell or Jerry Seinfeld in an average high school.

For example, picture the Sadie Hawkins dance. There is not that much plaid in one place outside of Scotland. Couples with their matching plaid shirts wear straw hats on their heads. Where else would girls put globs of eyeliner on their cheeks to imitate Daisy Mae freckles? Why would anyone deliberately put hay bales inside a building as a photo backdrop? Think of the 10-year class reunion when the classmates joke about how the hay poked them as they tried to sit still and smile for the camera. Do not forget the "preacher" who performs a "marriage" ceremony and gives a "marriage certificate." Where is the judge for the "divorce" ceremony?

Imagine Rosie or Jerry walking down the hall on a normal school day. Couples are so madly in love that they can barely stand to be parted from one another for a 50-minute class period. They linger until the bell rings, give each other a hurried "peck," and run to class as the bell quits ringing and the door closes. Think of the pulsing hormones. Imagine what the students are thinking about when they are supposed to be learning about past tense French verbs.

Adults in school are good material as well. Imagine a Second City parody of a staff meeting as the chronic nay-sayers complain once again about students parking in the staff lot while another teacher sits and tapes photography mats for the pictures in his photography class. Each time he pulls tape off the roll, the tape "quacks" almost in punctuating what the principal is saying.

Looking at the daily life of a school through the eyes of an outsider gives a perspective that can be quite humorous. When we look at our daily lives and take it all so seriously, it is as though we are looking through a window. We see and we act as though it were all so heavy. Humor is reflective, like a mirror. Looking with a sense of humor, as in a mirror, gives a perspective that is more like reflection. Events seem more removed, less onerous, and less intense.

When was the last time you really laughed so hard that your sides hurt? Can you even remember? Remember how good it felt after laughing? Laughter is a release, much like exercise or meditation. Belly laughs act as an "internal massage" that releases endorphins that in turn reduce stress and cause an increase in cancer-fighting capabilities, according to many people such as Norman Cousins (1979), in *Anatomy of an Illness*.

Educators tend to be a serious group, particularly at the secondary level. Elementary teachers are more likely to have fun and play with their students and each other. Junior high teachers have a reputation for being zany. The developmental stages of early adolescence are stressful and swing from mood to mood. If a teacher wants to stay sane in such an atmosphere, he or she must join in with the unpredictability. Junior high teachers tend to be the ones that dress up in gross costumes for Halloween. High school staff members may need to learn to be more playful.

The importance of smiling can be demonstrated to a class or a staff. Have a volunteer stand up, hold out an arm, and resist as someone else tries to push it down. Then draw a frowning face on the board and have the volunteer stare at it for 30 seconds. Then have him or her hold out the arm again and resist as someone pushes it down. The arm invariably collapses.

Next draw a happy face on the board. Have the volunteer stare at it for 30 seconds and then hold out an arm again. The arm will stay up. The volunteer will be able to describe the difference that their body felt during the experience. The happy face makes him or her feel better than the frowning face.

An observer would be able to watch the volunteer and describe a difference in body language. During the frowning face, shoulders slump, faces tense, and the mouth turns down at the corners. During the happy face segment, faces smooth out and hands relax.

There is power in positive thinking. Positive people seek out other positive people. Students request teachers who make them feel good. They seek out those with those happy faces. Research shows that stress decreases the ability to learn. The limbic system of the brain is put on alert when the organism is stressed, thereby cutting off the ability to retain information. Being upbeat and using humor increases the ability to learn.

A school community, like a family, needs staff get-togethers for the sheer fun of getting together. Administrators need to schedule times when the staff can play together and build the positive feelings of the group.

If life were a song, it should be reggae or calypso, not a dirge.

Suggestions for Shining the Mirror of Humor

1. Laugh. If you smile, people smile in return. If you frown, they frown in return.

2. Go to funny movies. There are a lot of films that are serious and violent on the market. Avoid them. Go see the films that promote healthy relationships and make people smile. There is enough of the traumatic at work every day.

3. Bring fresh flowers to work. The smell and the ambiance will change your outlook and the outlook of those who come to your office. They will believe that it is something special—and it is.

4. Learn to play. Do something frivolous.

8

Change Is Inevitable, Growth Is Optional

In the news each day, we hear about how life is changing rapidly with the technological revolution and information explosion. We know there are many sociological and political forces that affect schools. We know that our student populations are changing. We are seeing increased diversity with the blessings and problems that brings. We can no longer assume that the curriculum that we learned years ago is appropriate for our children. Curriculum must represent the populations we teach and must be sensitive to learning differences and language barriers.

Changes have come with inclusion. Special education laws have demanded that students with all types of handicaps must be included as much as possible, even if that means that a student has a full-time aide in the classroom. In the past, such students would be educated in special facilities where they would not be the concern of a classroom teacher. Unfortunately, many of our teachers feel unprepared and frightened of educating some of these students. They feel untrained, especially for any medical concerns.

Behaviorally, our students have changed. School is the last major cultural institution that everyone in our society experiences. Our culture used to assume certain support systems in a shared ethos that was taught and supported by family, church, and school. Now the last institutions to impart those values are our schools.

Some families have abdicated their responsibilities to the schools. Parents who do not discipline their children at home expect the school to do that. Some parents are afraid of their children, but the school is supposed to "fix" that.

Teachers and administrators alike feel beleaguered. Educational movements are coming faster and more frequently. Psychologically, we need time between ideas for transition, much like those stages described in Chapter 1. People need time to reflect and incorporate the old with the new. But if the transitions do not occur, if changes keep happening too quickly, there is not time to process.

Consequently, teachers and administrators are under a great deal of stress. It is as though there is nothing that is stable. Administrative training did not prepare us for dealing with such demands.

Three Personality Types in Dealing with Change

Change is inevitable. Much of it is productive. But if it comes too quickly, it can be destructive. How people deal with change is likely to fall into three categories.

- A Type One person will jump on the bandwagon and adopt anything new because our culture says "New is better." Some people like to be trendsetters, and they like the "high" of doing new things.

- A Type Two person may resist change because it comes too fast. They change only when absolutely forced into it.

- A Type Three uses a combination of approaches, sometimes changing readily and sometimes waiting. There are times when it is necessary to adopt a change quickly and other times when it is smart to wait.

We all have been part of educational trends that have come and gone within a few years. Within 15 to 20 years, an idea would recycle with a new name and twist. Today's world, however, has speeded up the process. For example, *competencies* was a buzzword in the early 1970s. The idea reappeared under the heading of Outcome-Based

Education in the 1980s. But when a public outcry arose, some schools officially dropped the jargon from their school profile, although they may still teach to outcomes.

In the 1990s, we have the Graduation Standards in Minnesota, another form of outcome-based education. Each student will have to be able to perform certain tasks in order to receive a high school diploma. Measurement of that performance may take many forms. The idea of having students demonstrate competency instead of being measured on seat-time has returned three times in a relatively short period.

Because the Grad Standards are a major change effort, many teachers are adopting a wait-and-see attitude. They say they will do what they have to do when they have to do it. They are not going to invest any effort or time until forced to do so, which is part of their resistance to rapid and complex change. They are Type Two teachers. It is their perception that those other ideas of competencies and OBE (Outcome-Based Education) came and did not change their classroom teaching so why should they invest in this idea because it probably will not make a difference either. Only when it is mandated that teachers demonstrate which outcomes a student has mastered in their class will they adapt. It will probably be done with much protest and whining.

The Type One teacher was one of the first teachers in the building to sit on committees to help shape what is called the Profiles in Learning. She or he may have helped write some of the assessments. She or he may be working at the State Department of Education during the summers to help decide which standards are appropriate.

The Type Three teacher is that person who acknowledges that the Grad Standards are coming, although they are still not in the final form. This teacher is reshaping some of his or her units to meet the performance assessments. She or he, however, has not redone everything because the Standards themselves are not finalized. This teacher will have some of the work done before the final Standards are implemented but will have to redo some things.

Humans need a certain constancy in their lives. When people have many changes in their personal lives, they may want their professional life to be stable. When their professional life is in flux, they will want stability in their personal life. If both areas are in turmoil, it is likely that one will see a person be ineffective and scattered in both areas. People such as Bernie Siegel, in his work with cancer patients, feel that such stress leads to illness and/or accidents.

Levels of Change

There are different levels of change within a building. First, there are the changes that are mandated by external organizations, such as the district office, the state department of education, and school boards. Such mandates are usually carried out to a degree. For example, districtwide testing has to be completed. The new process requires that, for each of their homeroom students, a teacher must make certain that all tests are completed with each student's name and number. If the teacher does not check that this is done accurately, someone else—usually a counselor—must do it. The counselor is overwhelmed because instead of checking 20 papers, she or he must check hundreds.

Because some teachers see this as one more thing they have to do, particularly as a noncurriculum chore, they resent being told what to do and will perform their task only minimally. They think that the process should be as it was in the past when the counselors were responsible for putting names and ID numbers on the forms. Even though this is a relatively small change, teachers resist because it is "just one more thing." It is the task of the administrator to deal with the resistance to change. Too many of these interferences undermine the morale of a staff.

Changes that come from external sources have a tendency to have little "buy-in" from teachers. The force initiating the change seems faceless and nameless, so there is no real connection. Some teachers do a wonderful job at whatever they are asked to do. There are many others who will perform such tasks at a minimum of compliance because there seems to be little about the change that involves the teacher. District decisions made without including teachers in the process fall into this category.

Another level is change in curricula and instructional delivery systems. This level affects individual teachers more directly. It is a combination of external force and internal need.

Because school was a successful place for most teachers, they may have difficulty delivering instruction in a mode that will accommodate different learning styles for divergent learners. Unless the teacher has had training, exhibits a great deal of empathy, or personally strives to understand how students learn, different modes of instruction and assessment may not appear in the classroom.

Effecting changes in the curriculum and delivery is often the topic of staff inservice and workshops. Because this is another change effort, there will be those who try to institute new ideas right away, others who adopt the wait-and-see attitude, and yet others who combine the two.

To make the level of change work, it is necessary to demonstrate how this change will improve learning for students and teaching for teachers. When a change is personally and professionally engaging, there is likely to be resistance.

A third level is internal changes that are created by personal needs. A teacher develops a new unit because she or he realizes that there is a better way to get information to students. Such changes are the most potent and immediate. Teachers learn quickly from other teachers. When there is strong motivation and payoff, a change is readily adopted.

Successful Change
Efforts in a Building

1. The key to making changes in a building is to make the efforts as internal as possible. To do that, it is necessary to know the culture of the building, its community, and the students. For example, some schools have students who are largely college-bound. Another building may have a higher percentage going to technical college, some to a 4-year college, and many getting a job. The emphasis for those two buildings would be different. What would be meaningful for one staff would not be for the other.

2. Involve as many stakeholders as possible in the process of deciding what should happen and how it should happen.

3. Bring in the nay-sayers too. For example, if the school is looking at block scheduling, form a committee of students, parents,

staff, and community to look at what the school needs and how other schools are using block scheduling. It is important to involve some of the strongest opponents on that committee to provide a voice. When opponents are involved, they change their opinion and become one of the strongest supporters. It is important to a staff to know that the committee was not "stacked" in favor of an issue.

4. Start small. For example, if an administrator wants more interdisciplinary teaching, start with one or two teams who are interested. Then, as their experience develops, have them share their experiences publicly at a staff meeting so that others stay informed.

If new ideas are working, they become contagious.

5. Provide time, training, and money for anyone willing to try. Time is the greatest gift to a teacher. If the scheduler can give teachers a common prep or if a teacher can be freed from a supervision responsibility to work on a new idea, then the teacher feels more rewarded for making an effort. New efforts should be promoted publicly several times a year in staff meetings so that the change becomes part of the group culture and inspires others to follow suit.

6. Provide ongoing support, in recognition, training, encouragement, and time.

A change effort is a lot like making sauerkraut. Cabbage is grated into large ceramic crocks. Every once in a while during the grating process, knuckles get scraped as well. After the cabbage is grated, salt is added. Then a weighted cover is put on top. The salt is to implement the fermentation process; the weight applies pressure to speed it up. The crock has to sit for a while. The process is working when it has a type of foam that bubbles up. It is also smelly.

Once the cabbage has fermented, it is sauerkraut, an entirely different product. It can be canned and then stored to be used at a different time, or it can be eaten immediately.

The change effort is a lot like that. The ideas are like the cabbage. They have to be modified—grated—and other parts added, like the salt, so that they can literally ferment. Pressure and patience must be applied before the change can occur. After time, the ideas take on a new life all their own. To some people, sauerkraut smells wonderful, to others it reeks. Some people welcome it, others hold their noses and walk away. Change is messy while in process but is appealing and positive to look back on.

Change Takes Time

The process of change, like fermentation, takes time. The first school year of any change effort is filled with excitement and mess. Ideas are explored. People may want to be a part of the effort.

In the second year, disillusionment often sets in. The newness has worn off. Sustained excitement takes energy. Many projects fall apart during this time because the problems surface and must be dealt with. It is important to offer ongoing support and recognition during this time for the effort to continue, because the effort is still not part of the overall school culture.

The third year is when things begin to gel. The problems have been dealt with, rewards can be seen, and other people begin to see the accomplishments. Recognition comes, and then the program becomes self-perpetuating. Many grants, unfortunately, are for 3 years, which means that many creative efforts are cut just as they are beginning to be part of the larger culture. The 3-year mark is when there needs to be a sustaining impetus to make the change effort become part of the school culture. Any new program needs 5 to 7 years to become truly integrated into the school culture. When funding is cut after 3 years, the effort is undermined at a crucial time.

Tasks of an Administrator in the Change Process

The primary function of the administrator is to set the focus and direction of the building. The efforts that support that direction may come from a variety of sources. Ideas often travel from the staff to the administration. Efforts may be mandated from the district. Ideas may come from the administrator personally in knowing what would work well in the building. A good administrator sets change in motion, then gets out of the way and lets the professionals do their job.

The second task of the administrator is to be the cheerleader and support for the change. Being a good support means that the administrator has to recognize where the effort is on the change timeline. Are they in the first year? Second? Third? Do the organizers need support, new ideas, or praise? Is it time for those involved to promote their efforts publicly?

The third task is to give recognition publicly and privately to those who are working hard. A good administrator will never take credit for the work of others. Public recognition has the function of exciting those on the outside to encourage them to join in, and it helps congeal the efforts of those involved. A public acknowledgment serves the same function as asking a student to sign a written contract, making it more likely that the effort will continue.

The fourth task is to build in continuity. Many administrators do not stay in their positions long enough to see their efforts mature. Teachers will be resistant to expend effort if they do not believe that there will be support for their efforts over a period of time. It takes 3 years to see real change mature; it takes 5 to 7 years for a change to become part of the culture. True change is not easy or fast. To be a change agent, it is important to commit to the long-term process.

Suggestions for Change

1. Recognize that change efforts take time. Understand that the first year is exciting, the second is difficult, and the third is the charm.

2. Because administration is inherently about change, it is important to keep one area in life in which there is certainty and constancy.

If there is much change in the personal realm, try to keep professional changes to a minimum.

The opposite is also true. If there are many professional changes, such as moving from one job to another, keep the personal changes to a minimum. For example, do not remodel your house the same time you accept a promotion.

3. Although some people are energized by change, too much of any one thing becomes negative. A drop of water is not enough to keep a geranium growing but a flood will kill it. A periodic rain shower keeps it alive and blooming.

9 | Power Is Like Love— The More You Give Away, the More You Have

Power and love are paradoxes. They are concepts about which people have an opinion. Although everyone knows what they are, it is difficult to agree about the definition.

Types of Power

In the hierarchy of schools, the ultimate power in the building rests with the principal. Each principal has a different interpretation of how to use this power. French and Raven (1959) defined five types of social power.

- *Reward power* is that which promises rewards if someone performs. Teachers earn more money if they get more credits.
- *Coercive power* is that which forces someone to act against their will. Teachers have to cover study hall even if they do not want to because it is a contractual agreement.
- *Legitimate power* is that which is assigned a certain position. Because the principal is in charge of the building, she or he can tell teachers what to do.
- *Referent power* is that which comes from a constituent's belief in the power of the superior. Hitler used his referent power to keep his SS guards from revolting.

- *Expert power* is that which comes from proficiency. If someone is the expert on authentic assessment in the building, that person has power. (pp. 155-164)

The historical authoritarian-father image of principal relied heavily on reward, coercive, and legitimate power. Principals could coerce staff and students to perform because cultural mores allowed it. He, and it usually was a he, was in charge. Subordinates were expected to follow the orders, and they did so with little challenge. In the past, it seemed that people were more accepting of the power that rests solely in position.

True leaders are able to motivate by the willingness of people to follow. Hence, a paradox. Leaders can lead only if others follow. To use an extreme example, cult leaders such as Hitler or James Jones would have had no power at all if people had not given it to them. If they had been ostracized as nutty radicals, they would have been marginalized and ineffective. However, people gave them power.

The type of leadership that works in today's schools relies on referent and expert power. Certainly, there is still reward power in operation. For example, the teachers who take on challenging roles are less likely to be asked to perform hall duty. If a teacher is the adviser to the yearbook, she may be given a sixth-hour prep. Those are definite rewards.

Referent power is exercised when teachers work with the principal because the principal is the boss. But referent power is often emotional. There are inspiring leaders whom people will follow without question. To be an effective principal, some of that awe of referent power is needed. Teachers are more likely to work hard with a principal they see as having personal strength, expertise, or charisma. Teachers are more likely to be passive-aggressive with a principal they see as ineffective, even if the person is still the "boss." It is an emotional process for the principal to use the referent power in drawing out the expertise of the staff, meshing it with the knowledge of the principal, and inculcating enthusiasm for change.

The principal also needs expert power. She or he needs to be an expert in daily pedagogy within a building and in global awareness of trends and best practices. Teachers expect a principal to understand the daily occurrences in a classroom. They also expect the principal to be intelligent, well-read, well-spoken, a good administrator, and creative.

Teachers want principals to use their *expert power* to perform the administrative tasks that facilitate a well-run building so that teachers can teach without being bogged down with time-consuming administrative tasks. Because most teachers love teaching, not politics and administration, site-based schools have difficulty getting teachers to take part. Teachers will say, "If I wanted to be an administrator, I'd be one. I don't want to do that. I want to teach! So keep me out of site councils."

When a principal walks the halls and tells tardy students to get to class and they do so, this is an example of *referent power* in action. If the students did not respect the person as principal, they would not move along.

Respect as Power

So much of what we mistake for power is actually respect. For example, an English teacher gives the students a 10-minute reading assignment. Most students are done in five. However, they sit quietly for the last five because they respect the teacher. This teacher has referent power. In a classroom directly across the hall with a different teacher who was not respected, those same students would have been talking or doing other homework. Their respect actually led to their own personal power by which they controlled their own actions.

Personal Power

Many people work hard to have power. They want a job at the top of the management flowchart so that they will be in charge. But most power is personal. Power attached to a position or title has severe limitations. Personal power is limitless. We each have all the power we need, if we choose to take it. I control my life because I want to. I accept responsibility for my actions because that is power.

Not taking responsibility for personal actions is a form of abdicating personal power. It is an old story that when one makes the gesture to point a finger at someone else, there are three fingers pointing back. The real responsibility lies with the individual.

As administrators, current leadership jargon includes the word *empowerment*. Books talk about empowering the staff or empowering the self. Change that word to *respect*. Respecting someone empowers them. When the English department wants to look at ways to improve reading, an administrator *respects* their work, provides opportunities and resources, and lets them work. That is empowerment.

It is a paradox that the more respect or power you give away, the more you will get in return. To use the same example, when the English teachers establish a concerted effort to do something about the reading levels of the students, their accomplishment is a reflection of a belief in them. The administrator "gave" them power to act professionally, they took it, and everyone won.

The idea of clutching power is an idea based in fear, fear of losing control, self-image, or self-worth. If buildings are administered from fear, there is constantly a sense of loss. If buildings are administered from a sense of worth and value, then there is a sense of general power and well-being.

Power Struggles

Power struggles are unnecessary. Parents come to the office embroiled in power struggles with their children. There is no way that anyone really wins in such a situation. One common issue is the defiance of curfew. If children want to stay out past curfew because they know that will really anger their parents, there is nothing that can stop the children from doing that. A child sets up a power struggle by defying a rule . The parent can be angry and administer punishment. When a child is at an age when he or she can make decisions such as abiding or not abiding curfew, such punishment is no longer effective.

Ultimately, what changes behavior is a sense of relationship between people. It is the respect that I have for you that gives you power over me. Power struggles ensue when there is a lack of respect between the parties. Someone cannot literally "make" their children come home on time unless they supervise them 24 hours a day. Children, however, will honor curfew if there is a meaningful, caring relationship that would be damaged by defying the rules.

Power struggles surface when someone feels scared or disadvantaged. They enter a contest with the mistaken perception that "winning" is important. But winning implies losing, which is what happens in a struggle. For example, a teacher told several students to be quiet in the hallway outside his door. They did not. He went out and yelled at them. They yelled back. He sent them to the office. They did not go. He called for help and a security guard was sent. The students then went to the office.

He never asked them to be quiet. He never related to them as responsible students. Instead, he ordered them to cooperate. When they did not, he "upped the ante." The students knew that their behavior was inappropriate. They did not have respect for the teacher, so they did not give him power over them. Instead, both parties escalated the problem, trying to win. The teacher, as adult, should have been smarter and not set up the struggle. He, literally, could not force them to be quiet or to move to the administration. The students happened to respect the security guard. They allowed the security guard to take them to the office. They could have run, fought, yelled, screamed, or been otherwise obnoxious, but they did not.

The teacher could have gone to the students and asked them to be quiet. He could have told the students that their noise was so loud that his students could not hear the morning announcements. He could have asked for their help instead of ordering them to be quiet. He could have used strategies that were based on relationships and caring about other people. Instead, he pushed, and they pushed back. He pushed again; they pushed back harder.

What would have worked better in this situation would have been for someone to sidestep the issue. Sometimes, when one person pushes on another person, he or she will be met with resistance. Force begets force. If, however, when the first person pushed, the other person moved aside, there would be nothing for the first person to push against. The struggle is defused. Asking for help is one way to defuse a situation. Using humor is another. Not responding to taunts is another. Adults need to examine the real issue and sidestep deliberate attempts at push and shove.

Power struggles never work because they are based on coercion and fear. Each of us has all the personal power we need.

Suggestions on How
to Disseminate Power

1. Give staff, students, and parents credit publicly and privately for what they do. The power of a staff is also the power of the administrator.

2. Sidestep power struggles. Look for the real issue and deal with it. Do not get involved when someone is having a bad day and taking it out on everyone around.

3. Power is more of a belief than a practice, just like love. Give it away in order to get it back.

10

Becoming a Self-Assured Administrator

Who said being an administrator would be fun? I did. It is an exciting position that affords one the opportunity to make a difference in a way that few people can. It is a career that helps shape our future. It is a job that allows a person the opportunity to continue learning and have fun doing it at the same time.

It is overwhelming because of the high expectations that are placed by the culture. An administrator is expected to be good in everything. People look to administrators for help as an expert. What an administrator is is a human in process of becoming.

There is no endpoint when the process will be DONE. Our society changes, our kids change, our schools change. Administrators will have to continue to be in the forefront of change and the effects of that change.

An administrator is seen as a super-communicator.

An administrator is supposed to know himself or herself so well that she or he can deal with personal feelings and the feelings of everyone else, particularly the staff.

An administrator is supposed to be the expert in education and policy. After all, teachers will say administrators "make the big bucks" in order to know all that.

What it means to be an administrator, however, is to be human above all. It is to enjoy life, learning, people. But most of all, it is to enjoy the PROCESS.

People who become tired in administration, whether in education or any other area, are those who become entangled in the endpoint of having attained the position, as opposed to remembering that the position is actually a job. It is fluid like a river. We keep flowing. We hit a few boulders now and then. The river must make a few turns and sometimes goes though deep gorges. Sometimes it freezes. But the water keeps coming.

Administration is trying, but it is never boring. It is a supreme opportunity to make a difference in the lives of students and staff. During an interview, someone once asked what one thing I wanted to do before the end of my career. The answer was that each year at graduation, I know that there are several students who could not walk across that stage if it were not for me. I want to keep doing that one thing as long as I can. That matters. That counts.

References

Bolman, L. G., & Deal, T. E. (1991). *Reframing organizations: Artistry, choice, and leadership.* San Francisco, CA: Jossey-Bass.

Cousins, N. (1979). *Anatomy of an illness.* New York: Bantam.

Cuban, L. (1996, March). *The framing and solving of problems.* Unpublished paper presented at Bush Educational Leadership Program, Minneapolis, MN.

Fishel, A., & Pottker, J. (1974). Women in educational governance: A statistical portrait. *Educational Researcher, 3*(7), 4-7.

Fisher, R., & Ury, W. (1991). *Getting to yes.* New York: Penguin.

French, J. R. P., & Raven, B. (1959). The bases of social power. In D. Cartwright (Ed.), *Studies of social power* (pp. 155-164). Ann Arbor: University of Michigan Press.

Hansot, E. W., & Tyack, D. B. (1981). *The dream deferred: A golden age for women school administrators.* Paper prepared for California Institute for Research on Educational Finance and Governance, Stanford University.

Jones, E. H., & Montenegro, X. P. (1990). *Women and minorities in school administration.* Arlington, VA: American Association of School Administrators.

Knowles, M. (1990). *The adult learner: A neglected species.* Houston: Gulf Publishing.

Kübler-Ross, E. (1969). *On death and dying.* New York: Touchstone.

Levinson, D. J. (1978). *The seasons of a man's life.* New York: Ballantine.

Lortie, D. C. (1975). *Schoolteacher: A sociological study.* Chicago: University of Chicago Press.

Nickerson, N. (1993). Secondary School Administator Course, University of Minnesota.

Paddock, S. C. (1980). Women principals: The rule or the exception. *NASSP Bulletin, 64*(440), 1-4.

Shakeshaft, C. (1989). *Women in educational administration.* Newbury Park, CA: Corwin Press.

Peck, M. S. (1978). *The road less traveled.* New York: Simon & Schuster.

Shakeshaft, C. (1987). Theory in a changing reality. *Journal of Educational Equity and Leadership, 7*(1), 4-20.

Sheehy, G. (1976). *Passages: Predictable crises of adult life.* New York: E. P. Dutton.

Sigford, J. L. (1995). *Self-determinants of success by the women who are head principals of high schools in Minnesota.* Unpublished doctoral dissertation, University of Minnesota, Minneapolis, MN.

Tyack, D. B., & Strober, M. H. (1981). *Women and men in the schools: A history of the sexual structuring of educational employment.* Paper prepared for the National Institute of Education, Washington DC.

Ury, W. (1991). *Getting past no: Negotiating with difficult people.* New York: Penguin.

CORWIN
PRESS

The Corwin Press logo—a raven striding across an open book—represents the happy union of courage and learning. We are a professional-level publisher of books and journals for K–12 educators, and we are committed to creating and providing resources that embody these qualities. Corwin's motto is "Success for All Learners."